Portraits of the
Spirit-Filled Personality

Portraits of the Spirit-Filled Personality

Guidelines for Holy Living from Philippians

A.B. Simpson

Christian Publications
Camp Hill, Pennsylvania

Christian Publications
3825 Hartzdale Dr, Camp Hill, Pennsylvania

Faithful, biblical publishing since 1883

ISBN: 0-87509-655-7
LOC Catalog Card Number: 95-83830
© 1996 by Christian Publications, Inc.
All rights reserved.
Printed in the United States of America.

96 97 98 99 00 5 4 3 2 1

Portraits of the Spirit-Filled Personality
was formerly published under the title
Sweetest Christian Life.

CONTENTS

INTRODUCTION

The epistle to the Philippians is an inspired delineation of the Christian temper. While Ephesians describes the highest Christian life, Philippians portrays the sweetest Christian life. It deals not so much with the essential elements of holy character as the finer quality of these elements.

The difference between that exquisite hairspring in a costly watch, more valuable than the same weight in gold, and the rough bar of pig iron, is wholly in the temper. They are both iron, but the one is exquisitely refined and the other is coarse and crude. The difference between that flashing diamond that blazes like a coal of celestial fire and the common lump of coal that you throw into your furnace, is merely a question of temper. They are both carbon, but the one is refined carbon polished and cut into flashing facets of light and beauty, while the other is common, rough coal. The difference between the ordinary tombstone that you can buy for a few dollars in the marble shop, and the classic bust by Michelangelo worth hundreds of thousands of dollars, lies not in the material but in the finer touches of genius and

1

art. It is all a matter of quality. The difference between the crabapple that falls from the apple tree
by the roadside and the perfectly developed and
exquisitely flavored pippin, is of the same character.

And these are all but feeble illustrations of the
infinite difference in the religious character and
the divine workmanship of the Holy Spirit in
molding human hearts and lives. There are infinite degrees of progress in the refining and sancti-
fying work of the Holy Spirit, and this epistle
leads us out into the less ordinary lines of holy
character and spiritual culture. Let us not be surprised if we find many of these qualities lacking in
us, because they are not ordinary qualities, but let
us press on to their attainment and realization by
the grace of Jesus Christ, as we learn in all its
length and breadth and depth and height, to have
in us the same mind which was also in Christ Jesus (Philippians 2:5).

It was peculiarly fitting that this exquisite epistle should have been written to the church in
Philippi. This was the first of the European
churches planted by the early missionaries. This
was the pioneer of that glorious chain of Christian
congregations which form part of the ecclesiastical
succession. Looking down through the coming
ages, the Holy Spirit called the apostles to leave
the continent of Asia and plant the gospel in
Europe which was to be the seat of the history of
the coming centuries. And so we have a peculiar
interest in this mother church of the European na-

tions. It was always very true to Paul, and out of these close and affectionate ties, as a sort of exquisite environment, there grew ideals and conceptions of truth and life which could not have been developed in colder or less tender associations. It is in the genial climate and the tropical atmosphere of love that we get our highest thoughts of God and godliness. And it was to the people who loved so tenderly that the greatest heart that ever throbbed since Christ's ascension brought out these tender messages of heavenly truth and love.

CHAPTER 1

The Christian Temper as Exemplified and Illustrated in Paul

I have you in my heart.
(Philippians 1:7)
For to me, to live is Christ and to die is gain.
(1:21)

The first chapter of Philippians gives us a portrait of the apostle's own heart and character. It is drawn by his own hand. Yet he is free from egotism, and even unconscious of himself while so fully unfolding his inmost heart. It is possible for us to reveal ourselves in perfect transparency, and yet have no thought of ourselves at all, even as a little child most completely reveals himself and yet most completely forgets himself. A letter has this advantage over a sermon, in that it lets out the heart of the writer, and the teachings of the New Testament are not sermons or homilies, but letters of affection.

Paul's Spirit

1. The first trait that strikes us in this sketch is

the affectionateness of Paul's spirit. Sanctification does not take out of our hearts the spirit of tenderness and love. It purifies and intensifies every heartstring. "I have you in my heart" (1:7), he says, and "God can testify how I long for all of you with the affection of Christ Jesus" (1:8).

The very cords of his sensitive being were alive with tender yearning; for these beloved friends are children in the Lord. The nearer we get to Christ the nearer we get to Christian people, and the tenderer is every holy tie. And so in that exquisite picture of consecration that he has given us in the 12th chapter of Romans we find such passages as this, "Be kindly affectioned one to another with brotherly love" (12:10, KJV). And here we find him saying a little later, "If you have any encouragement from being united with Christ, if any comfort from his love, if any fellowship with the Spirit, if any tenderness and compassion, then make my joy complete by being like-minded, having the same love, being one in spirit and purpose" (Philippians 2:1–2).

Christian Fellowship

2. Christian fellowship is next recognized, especially in connection with his relations to his beloved Philippian brethren. There are some natures that are coldly isolated and independent. They naturally and instinctively stand apart in their joys and sorrows, refusing to open their petals to the sunshine of love, and dwelling in a little world of their own. This is not the genius of Christianity,

nor was it the spirit of Paul. His heart was open as the full-blown rose, giving and receiving the sweetness and fragrance of love in relation to all. And so he speaks with the deepest thankfulness of their "partnership in the gospel from the first day until now" (1:5), and adds with deep appreciation of their sympathy and help, "Whether I am in chains or defending and confirming the gospel, all of you share in God's grace with me" (1:7). He recognizes their help to him and he rejoices in his power to be a blessing to them. God has thus linked us one to the other even as the members of the human body are linked by joints and ligaments, and made us members one of another so that we can share each other's blessings, we can feel each other's sufferings, we can enrich each other's experience. Christian fellowship is God's ordinance, and every true heart should be able to join in the ancient creed with true wholehearted fullness, "I believe in the communion of saints."

The Spirit of Cheer, Hope and Thanks

3. The next quality we note in this portraiture is the spirit of cheerfulness, hopefulness and thankfulness. There is no depression about it. There is no reproachfulness about it. There is no shadow of discontent, criticism or gloom, but it is all appreciation, thankfulness and confidence. "I thank my God every time I remember you" (1:3). The very recollection of them brings pleasure to him; and as he looks forward to their future he has no premonitions, doubts or fears, but he can say,

"Being confident of this, that he who began a good work in you will carry it on to completion until the day of Christ Jesus" (1:6).

This is a beautiful quality in Christian character. There are some people who make us tired by their concern for us, their fears for our future, their criticisms of our faults. If Paul had any suggestion to make to his brethren he always first bathed them in an ocean of love and then they hardly knew that he was even criticizing. In one of his most beautiful passages he bids us to "admonish one another with all wisdom, and as you sing psalms, hymns and spiritual songs" (Colossians 3:16). Sing to our friends our counsels and admonitions rather than scold them.

We find this in a very marked way in the epistles of our Lord to the seven churches in Asia. His first word is always commendation, and after He has recognized at their full value the things that are excellent, He then tells them of the things that should be changed. God give us the love that "always trusts, always hopes," as well as "always perseveres" (1 Corinthians 13:7).

Unselfish Prayer

4. We next note the spirit of unselfish prayer for his brethren. In all this epistle we do not find Paul offering a single prayer for himself. In fact, he tells them a little later that he has no needs, "I have received full payment and even more; I am amply supplied" (Philippians 4:18). He has enough to give away, and his one thought is to

bless others. We find him praying for them with every breath and every remembrance, "In all my prayers for all of you, I always pray with joy" (1:4).

And yet his prayer is not a mere redundancy of words or emotions. It is an intelligent, discriminating, positive and most helpful petition for real things, things that they actually need. "And this is my prayer," he says, "that your love may abound more and more in knowledge and depth of insight, so that you may be able to discern what is best and may be pure and blameless until the day of Christ" (1:9–10). He wants them to have real and very definite blessings, to be clear-cut in their character and experience, and to reach the highest possibilities of Christian perfection, so that in the day of Christ he may be able to present them blameless and harmless, and may rejoice that he has not run in vain, neither labored in vain.

Victorious Faith

5. Then there is the spirit of victorious faith over difficulties and trials. His was no soft, effeminate character languidly developed by easy, sentimental associations, but it was disciplined in the sturdy conflict of adversity and suffering. As he wrote these exquisite lines of courage, thankfulness and love, he was himself a prisoner in the Roman barracks, sleeping every night between two soldiers, and waiting to be brought before a cruel and wicked judge to be tried for his life. Yet he is so afraid that they may be discouraged by his difficulties that he

hastens to have them understand that "what has happened to me has really served to advance the gospel" (1:12), and that his very bonds and afflictions have really led to more glorious results for the Master's cause. The soldiers that have been chained to him have been converted through his influence, and the brethren that were timid before have been encouraged by his brave example to give a bolder testimony for Christ. None of his trials move him or even depress him for a moment, but he rises supreme above them all in the singleness of his desire to glorify his Master. Brave, glorious spirit, undaunted, unintimidated, not discouraged by the persecutions of earth or the hate of hell, shining like a glowing star the brighter for the darkness around him, blooming like a sweet rose amid the glaciers of the Alps, "sorrowful, yet always rejoicing; poor, yet making many rich; having nothing, and yet possessing everything" (2 Corinthians 6:10).

Victory Over People

6. Next there is victory over people. More trying even than circumstances, are human hearts, natures out of sympathy with us, souls that seem especially adjusted to irritate, lacerate and rasp our most sensitive feelings.

Paul speaks of some who "preach Christ out of envy and rivalry" (Philippians 1:15), and, under the very guise of goodness and service, aim only to humiliate and injure him. It is very hard to rise superior to people who misrepresent our best endeavors, oppose us in our holiest efforts and in the very name of religion are but emissaries of hate and evil. But Paul could stand even this so long as they preached Christ. Though it were for "contention," and in "pretense," he could say, "The important thing is that in every way, whether from false motives or true, Christ is preached. And because of this I rejoice" (1:18). If the Master was glorified, if the truth was spread, if the gospel was made known, that was his one concern and his supreme satisfaction. Surely this is a nature larger, nobler than all the petty jealousies and rivalries of sects and parties. The thought may well cover with a blush of shame many who have used even their Christian work as a means of self-glorification or the gratification of bigotry, prejudice and controversy.

Devotion to Christ

7. Next, Paul's devotion to Christ stands out. The secret of all this was his single-hearted devotion to Jesus Christ. The one thing he cared for, lived for, and was willing to die for, was that "Christ shall be magnified in my body whether it be by life, or by death" (1:20, KJV), and the one illustrious sentence in which he emblazons it forth like a passion sign of love is this immortal epigram, "For to me, to live is Christ and to die is gain" (1:21). This is the secret of every glorious soul and every earnest life: intense, fervid devotion to the Lord Jesus Christ. It was the one ambition of Paul's life, and like a great volcanic torrent it swept away everything in its current, transfused everything into its own burning flame, and made

him the bond slave of Jesus Christ. "For Christ's love compels us" (2 Corinthians 5:14). It was not living for Christ, but it was living for Christ alone.

Holy Indifference

8. Paul displayed a holy indifference. His supreme motive of love to Christ raised him above every selfish preference and enabled him to care little for gain or loss, life or death for their own sakes. When he stopped to think whether he preferred to live or die, he was at a loss to determine. Personally he preferred to go and be with Christ, and yet when he thought of his work and his brethren he longed to remain with them. He was in that state of mind where the world could neither attract him nor distract him. Like General Gordon, when the Mahdi threatened him with death, he smiled and said, "You could not do me a greater favor than thus quickly to introduce me into the presence of my best Friend, and the enjoyment of highest reward." Such men have nothing to lose, nothing to gain, nothing to fear. Life has found a perfect equilibrium by being poised from the center and fixed forever on its true axis in devotion to Christ alone.

Sublime Confidence

9. Paul had a sublime confidence. His very indifference gave him faith. Because he did not care for life for its own sake, he knew that he should live, and was able to claim it, not for himself, but for Christ and for others; and so he could add,

"Convinced of this, I know that I will remain, and I will continue with all of you for your progress and joy in the faith" (Philippians 1:25).

The way to have faith for healing is to give up your life for Christ, and then take it back from Christ for Christ. While we want even life for its own sake, we shall not be able to believe for it; but when it ceases to be our own and becomes a consecrated trust for Him, then we can say with Paul "I know that I will remain, and I will continue" (1:25) until our life work is done.

Thus we have glanced all too briefly at the unconscious portrait which this simple-hearted yet glorious saint has given of his own heart and life. His qualities as we have already said are not ordinary qualities. They represent a very high plane of Christian experience. We shall find the secret of them in the next chapter, "Your attitude should be the same as that of Christ Jesus" (2:5).

It is a comfort to know that not only has this life once been lived by Christ, but it has also been lived by Paul. It is not only a divine pattern but it has been a human experience. Not only has the Son of man walked through the path of time in these beautiful habits of loveliness and grace, but another man, animated with His Spirit, united to His life and exposed to all the trials and hindrances which could beset a human existence, has trod the same path and has passed on to a triumph unsullied by failure and a glory unalloyed and everlasting. Let us not be slothful, "But . . . imitate those who through faith and patience inherit what has been promised" (Hebrews 6:12). Let us look at our shortcomings and failures in the light of these sublime examples, and then sinking into the nothingness of our insufficiency, let us claim His all-sufficiency and let Him live out in us His own victorious life, even as He lived it in this blessed pattern man who speaks to us down through the ages, "Follow my example, as I follow the example of Christ" (1 Corinthians 11:1).

CHAPTER 2

The Christian Temper as Exemplified in Christ

Your attitude [mind, KJV] should be the same as that of Christ Jesus. (Philippians 2:5)

Every great creation must have an archetype and pattern. Many a waiting year and many a patient effort are spent in perfecting the model of some marvelous invention which is to revolutionize modern mechanics or industrial art. After the model is made it is not hard to reproduce it in millions of copies. It is the first machine that counts. The others are but copies.

God spent 4,000 years showing the inadequacy of all human types of character. Then, after an Adam, an Abraham, a Moses, a David and even an Elijah had failed, He revealed the Man for whom the ages had been waiting, the perfect Pattern and Type of human character, by which all others were to be molded and fashioned. As He looked upon Him on the banks of the Jordan He exclaimed in approving love, "You are my Son, whom I love; with you I am well pleased" (Luke 3:22). Henceforth all redeemed men are to be conformed to that divine Pattern, the image of His Son, the Firstborn among many brethren.

Christ's Character and Example

Even Paul is a secondary example, and we are to follow him only as he followed Christ. All other lights are but reflected lights receiving their illumination from Him, and shedding it in return on others. With glowing love and admiration the apostle proceeds to delineate His heavenly character and example.

1. Conscious Dignity

The conscious dignity of Christ is the starting point of the description. While it is a picture of humility and voluntary humiliation, yet it begins with a height of glory transcendently beyond any human character. He was "in very nature God" (Philippians 2:6). The language has the force and bears the construction that He was equal with God, that He was a possessor of the very nature of God, was Himself a divine Person. It was because of His high dignity and His consciousness of it that He was able to stoop so low. It is the lofty character that is able to condescend, while the person ambitious of vain display and earthly honor is always trying to hold up the little reputation he has. One of true rank is easily indifferent to outward appearances because he knows that his dignity cannot be questioned, and mere adventitious circumstances cannot take it away.

This is very strikingly illustrated in the 13th chapter of John in the account of the washing of the disciples' feet. It was because Jesus knew that He came from God and went to God, that without any thought of His own honor or dignity, He rose from supper and immediately began to wash the disciples' feet and to wipe them with the towel with which He was girded.

And so, before we can imitate Christ's example of humility, we must know our high calling and heavenly dignity as the sons of God. Then it will not be hard to stoop to the lowest depths of self-abasement and self-sacrifice.

2. *Voluntary Surrender*

The translation of the next clause is a little unfortunate. He "thought it not robbery to be equal with God" (Philippians 2:6, KJV), has been rendered by the common consent of scholars, "did not consider equality with God something to be grasped." He did not hold on to His rights and honors, but willingly yielded them. It was His rights that He yielded, the things that He might have retained, and no one ever questioned His holding to His high prerogative. But He suspended His deity for a time and took the place of a servant and a man.

3. *Complete Surrender*

Not only did He give up something but He gave up all. "But made himself nothing" (2:7) is better rendered, "He emptied himself." He let all go like Boaz, who sacrificed his own inheritance and family name and became merged into the family of Ruth because he loved her. So Jesus Christ became a part of humanity and is forever known in heaven as a man.

4. Surrendered Will

Jesus surrendered His own will. This is the last thing we let go. Man would rather be a king in a cottage than a servant in a palace. But Jesus, who had created all things and ruled the whole creation, stooped to be a servant in His own world—to be controlled by His Father's will and the will of others; to hold Himself in constant subjection to the people around Him; to comfort the disciples who leaned upon Him and claimed Him as a brood of children would a fond mother; even to submit to the very enemies that at last deprived Him of His liberty and His life. And He yielded all, step by step, sacrifice by sacrifice, until at last He was "led like a lamb to the slaughter,/ and as a sheep before her shearers is silent,/ so he did not open his mouth" (Isaiah 53:7). Like Him, the Christian temper enables us to yield our personal will, to be subject one to another in the fear of God and to count ourselves the servants of God, waiting on His bidding, listening to His word and surrendering all to His supreme command.

5. His Earthly Position

Lower still He descended, to be found not only

in fashion like a man but the lowest of men, the humblest of the race. He was not a child of wealth or royalty or honor, but was born among the poor and lowly, and of a maiden mother, whose peculiar situation even threw upon His birth a shadow of suspicion and dishonor.

6. Obedient to Death

And even this lowly and humble lot was at last surrendered, when He "became obedient to death" (Philippians 2:8), and gave up His very life in complete sacrifice for the world's redemption.

7. His Final Sacrifice

His final sacrifice was rendered as humbling, as painful and as full of reproach and shame as it was possible. It was no heroic death. It was no illustrious tragedy. It was no such passing out of existence as the military hero whose fame is chronicled to latest ages; but it was as a criminal, as the scum of the world that Jesus died. Carried outside the city gate as one vile enough to defile the whole precincts of Jerusalem by His execution, crucified between two thieves as if He were a common convict, and buried at last in a stranger's grave, the death of Christ was as humbling as His life had been, and His sacrifice was made complete from beginning to end.

There are thousands of people who are willing to make a sacrifice and to do some heroic things if it brings them distinction. Men are dying today by hundreds on the battlefield, and proud and glad to have the honor of winning an illustrious name. If there can be something dramatic in our trials, some heroic luster, some halo of earthly fame, human nature will stoop to the very depths of sacrifice.

> Man for man will boldly brave
> The terrors of the yawning grave;
> And friend for friend, and child for sire
> Undaunted and unmoved expire
> For love or piety or pride;
> But who can die as Jesus died?

And yet this was the character of ancient martyrdom. The men and women who suffered in the Roman Colosseum were not slain as heroes of the faith, but as pests of society. Gentle women were charged with the basest crimes, treated with the foulest outrage, and cast to the wild beasts as monsters of iniquity; they knew that they had no glory in the minds of men for heroism or even decency.

And so, beloved, if you step out with your Master to humiliation and sacrifice, do not be surprised if the world misunderstands you, and if even the very people that call themselves Christians often misjudge your motives and character. The cross was not only painful but shameful, and the tests of Christian character which God gives will lead us all the way to Calvary. But if we have learned our high and heavenly dignity, we shall be so possessed with "the joy set before" us (Hebrews 12:2), and the vision of His glory, that "scorning its shame" (12:2), we shall not fear the reproach, we shall not shrink from humiliation; but we shall rather rejoice that we are "counted worthy of suffering disgrace for the Name" (Acts 5:41).

More Than a Pattern

Such is the picture of the divine Pattern. But it is much more than a pattern, more than an example, more than a standard for our imitation. One of the greatest books written is *The Imitation of Christ*. It is indeed a sublime theme, the work of a master spirit, and worthy of its circulation as the most widely published book in the world except the Holy Scriptures themselves. But the human heart unaided cannot imitate Christ any more than the canary can imitate Patti [an Italian operatic soprano] or the babe can imitate a giant.

Christ is more than a Pattern to us, more than a bright and glorious Example. He becomes the Power to reproduce that pattern and to transfer to our lives that example. Our text does not bid us to imitate Christ or have a mind like Him, but to have the *same* mind in us which was also in Christ Jesus. This is the deepest truth of all Christian experience. It is Christ Himself who comes to imitate Himself in us and reproduce His own life in the lives of His followers. This is the mystery of the gospel. This is the secret of the Lord. This is the power that sanctifies, that fills, that keeps the consecrated heart. This is the only way that we can be like Christ. And so we change the little song:

> Give me a heart like Thine;
>> By Thy wonderful power,
>> By Thy grace every hour
> Give me a heart like Thine.

to:

> Give me Thy heart in mine;
>> By Thy wonderful power,
>> By Thy grace every hour
> Give me Thy heart in mine.

The word "let" expresses the whole idea of the divine life. It is not our doing but His. We do not accomplish it, but we let Him live out His life within us. It is the "expulsive power of a new affection." It is the divine transcending the human. It is the "I no longer live, but Christ lives in me" (Galatians 2:20). Even the teachers of holiness are in danger of substituting holiness for Him, a clean heart for the divine nature. The mystery of godliness is "Christ in you, the hope of glory" (Colossians 1:27).

The end of all experience is union with God. God has made everything for Himself, and the heart never rests till it receives Him and draws all its life from Him. Just as the flower needs the sunshine, and all its exquisite tints are but the outshining of the light that has first shone in, so the graces of the Christian life are but the reflection of the Christ who dwells within. Redemption is not the restoration of fallen man, but the new creation of a redeemed family under the headship of the second Adam on an infinitely higher plane than even unfallen humanity could ever have reached alone. "As was the earthly man, so are those who are of the earth; and as is the man from heaven, so also are those who are of heaven" (1 Corinthians 15:48). We are first born of the Christ, then united to Him, just as Eve was formed out of her husband, and then wedded to him. The redeemed soul is formed out of the Savior, and then united to Him in an everlasting bond of love and unity, more intimate than any human relationship can ever express.

It is not by a figure that Christ lives in us, in the sense of His truth, the ideas which He has inculcated in the gospel, or the influences which He brings to bear upon us. The message of godliness is nothing less than this: that the very person of Jesus is revealed to and formed in the sanctified soul, and our whole Christian life henceforth is a putting on of Christ and taking from Him moment by moment each grace that we need to live it out, so that it is literally true that "in him we live and move and have our being" (Acts 17:28).

Do we want humility? We receive the spirit of humility from Him, and let the same mind be in us which was also in Him. Do we want love? We open our hearts for a baptism of His love and it flows into us and lives through us. Do we want patience, courage, wisdom, anything? We simply put on the Lord Jesus, and "Your attitude should be the same as that of Christ Jesus" (Philippians 2:5).

Does this destroy our individuality and make each of us simply an automation without will or responsibility? Certainly not. So perfect is the divine adjustment to our human nature, so delicately does God recognize in us the power of choice and the right of personal liberty, that He will not come until we invite Him, and He will not act except as we cooperate by constant yielding and receiving. The slightest hesitation on our part to follow will check His grace. He will not force Himself into our life, but He will meet the surrendered will and fill the heart that opens all its being to receive Him. Just as the flower is made to receive the sun and only reaches its individuality when filled with sunshine; just as the soil needs the rain and the seed, and only accomplishes the purpose of its being when it receives the seed and absorbs the rain; so the human heart is made for Christ and it is incomplete until it receives Him. He is the complement of its being, and it unfolds and blossoms into all its predestined powers when quickened by His life, and inspired by His presence, and planted and watered by His indwelling life and love.

The 15th chapter of the Gospel of John is perhaps the most perfect unfolding of this message of the abiding life. The three keynotes are "in him," "in us," and "abide." We are not to struggle. We are not to try. We are not to do. We are not to be. We are simply to let Him be and so abide that His life shall flow through us as the sap flows through the branches of the vine, and the rich clusters hang without an effort through the spontaneous life which flows through all the beautiful organism of the plant.

The word "mind" (Philippians 2:5, KJV) here employed suggests that this is not only a spiritual experience but that it is also designed for our intellectual life, for our mental being, for our thoughts, affections, emotions and all the sensibilities of the soul as well as the spirit. Indeed, we have learned that it includes the body too, and there is no power of our redeemed humanity which this blessed Christ cannot fill, and of which He is not fitted to be the fountain of life, and the source of all our power, and the supply of all our need.

What an exquisite simplicity this gives to Christian life. It takes all the complications out of it. It is not a thousand things we have to do, but one. We are occupied with Him, and He takes care of us. We are not watching ourselves and keeping ourselves in constant strain, but we are sweetly abiding in Him. And just as the water flows from the fountain into all the pipes, just as the law of gravitation goes out from the sun to the smallest world that circles in its orbit around that central sun, so while we are attached to Him and in touch with Him it is true every moment, "Because I live, you also will live" (John 14:19). Thus we find such expressions as this, especially in the writings of Paul and John: "I can do everything through him who gives me strength" (Philippians 4:13). "No one who lives in him keeps on sinning" (1 John 3:6). "From the fullness of his grace we have all received one blessing after another" (John 1:16). "The life I live in the body, I live by faith in the Son of God, who loved me and gave himself for me" (Galatians 2:20).

In conclusion let us behold the divine Pattern in all its beauty and completeness, until it humbles us in the dust with the sense of our own failure. Then let us turn to the divine Original, and opening our hearts, receive Him with loving surrender and constant dependence. Thus shall this "mind be in [us] which was also in Christ Jesus" (Philippians 2:5, KJV).

CHAPTER 3

The Christian Temper as Illustrated in the Friends of Paul

I have no one else like him, who takes a genuine interest in your welfare. For everyone looks out for his own interests, not those of Jesus Christ. But you know that Timothy has proved himself, because as a son with his father he has served with me in the work of the gospel. (Philippians 2:20–22)

But I think it is necessary to send back to you Epaphroditus, my brother, fellow worker and fellow soldier, who is also your messenger, whom you sent to take care of my needs. For he longs for all of you and is distressed because you heard he was ill. Indeed he was ill, and almost died. But God had mercy on him, and not on him only but also on me, to spare me sorrow upon sorrow. Therefore I am all the more eager to send him, so that when you see him again you may be glad and I may have less anxiety. Welcome him in the Lord with great joy, and honor men like him. (2:25–29)

27

There is no brighter galaxy of beautiful lives than the cluster of friends that circled around the Apostle Paul. Their personality stands out in bold relief in his various epistles. The figures of Aquila and Priscilla, Silas and Barnabas, Tychicus and Trophimus, Onesiphorus and Epaphroditus, Timothy and Titus, Luke and even Mark, stand out as familiar friends. Their relations with the great apostle were most intimate, affectionate and helpful. With a heart peculiarly sensitive and loving, his whole being was open to every tie of holy friendship, and the glimpses his letters give us of these sacred friendships are full of the rarest touches of lofty character and nobility.

Two special pictures are given in the texts we have quoted.

Timothy, or the Loyal Helper

The relation of Timothy to Paul was filial. "To Timothy, my true son in the faith" (1 Timothy 1:2) was Paul's usual salutation to his beloved disciple. Converted to God through the ministry of Paul, adopted by him from the beginning of his Christian life as his disciple, companion and helper, and associated with him till the very close of the apostle's career in the most intimate and confidential relations, he could say of him, "I have no one else like him, who takes a genuine interest in your welfare. For everyone looks out for his own interests, not those of Jesus Christ. But you know that Timothy has proved himself, because as a son with his father he has served with me in the work of the gospel" (Philippians 2:20–22).

1. Timothy was a helper.

It is not easy to take the second place. It needs more grace to be a good helper than a good principal. There are plenty of people who are willing to take a subordinate place for a time to serve some ultimate ambition, but it takes a rare quality of humility and devotion to fit into second place and live to carry out the plans and objects which another has originated. And yet this is the true spirit of the New Testament. "You know that the rulers of the Gentiles lord it over them . . . Not so with you. Instead, whoever wants to become great among you must be your servant, and whoever wants to be first must be your slave" (Matthew 20:25–27). One of the most successful of modern missionaries went to the field in the first instance as a body-servant of a missionary, and God honored him afterwards equally with his former master and made the name of Marshman immortal among the records of noble lives. "[m]y fellow workers in Christ Jesus" (Romans 16:3). This clause included many of the noblest lives in apostolic times. This is the trust that is given to most of us. May God make us true "helpers in Christ Jesus."

2. Timothy was a truehearted and loyal helper.

In every age truth and honor have been counted

sacred, and treachery base. The ethics of Christianity give no lower place to loyalty, and among the signs of the declension and apostasy of the last days, are mentioned "trucebreakers" (2 Timothy 3:3, KJV) and "covenantbreakers" (Romans 1:31, KJV). A man who will be false to his fellow man will also prove recreant to his trust and to his God, if the temptation and inducement are only sufficiently strong. Let us ask God to make us true to every trust.

3. Timothy was an unselfish and disinterested helper and fellow-worker.

Paul had found few such helpers. Even in apostolic days men used the Christian ministry to further selfish ends. "For everyone looks out for his own interests, not those of Jesus Christ" (Philippians 2:21). "I have no one else like him, who takes a genuine interest in your welfare" (2:20). But here was one truehearted shepherd who only desired the good of the flock and the things that would please the Chief Shepherd. It was more than human friendship; it was more than loyalty to a leader; it was more than zeal for a cause—it was a love for souls that "takes a genuine interest in your welfare" (2:20). It was the heart of the Master in the minister, pitying, sympathizing, entering into the very needs and conditions of the flock and caring for them even as Christ would care. Without this there can be no true service. "What I want is not your possessions but you" (2 Corinthians 12:14), the true-hearted apostle could say. And so every true minister of Christ should be filled with the unselfish love, the disinterested aim, the shepherd heart—the very affection of Jesus Christ—toward the people for whom he stands in the Master's name. All others are but hirelings. These only are the true under-shepherds of the sheep.

Epaphroditus, or the Considerate Friend

The story of Epaphroditus is unique. He belonged to the church in Philippi, and was sent to Rome by the Philippian church while Paul was there in prison. He was probably one of the elders or pastors of the Philippian church. Hearing of the apostle's sufferings, he made strenuous exertions to find him out and minister to him, and through his violent over-exertions, he became ill himself, dangerously ill. But so unselfish was he that he took special pains to conceal the knowledge of his sickness from his friends in Philippi lest they should be anxious about him. And when at length he found that they had heard the tidings he was "distressed" (Philippians 2:26) because they had heard that he had been sick. At length, however, God graciously restored him to health and spared the apostle the bitter sorrow which his death would have caused him, and Paul now sends him back to the Philippians as the bearer of this epistle and commends him to their confidence and love as one who "for the work of Christ, [risked] his life to make up for the help you could not give me" (2:30).

There are some exquisitely fine touches of character in this picture:

1. Epaphroditus had the spirit of service.

Epaphroditus had gone from Philippi to Rome to carry to Paul the gifts of the Philippian Christians and to assist the apostle in his work. And Paul speaks of him as "My brother, fellow worker and fellow soldier, who is also your messenger, whom you sent to take care of my needs" (2:25).

He was undoubtedly a spiritual worker, and able to minister Christ to the souls of men. But he was not above the humblest ministration of help to the bodies of men. He carried with his own hands the gifts of his brethren to the lone apostle at Rome, and doubtless ministered personally with lowly service to his physical necessities. Are we ministering to Christ's suffering ones? Are we seeking out His poor, His sick, His prisoners, and doing it as unto Him?

2. Epaphroditus had the spirit of sacrifice.

Such was Epaphroditus' spirit of sacrifice that he risked his very life to minister to Paul. He toiled and traveled till he became exhausted and ill. He went beyond his strength. He lingered in the cold barracks or the damp dungeon until he contracted malignant disease and "almost died" (2:30). He did it willingly, "risking his life" (2:30). He was glad to sacrifice as well as serve for the sake of his Master and his friend.

Beloved, how much have you sacrificed for

Christ? How often have you risked your health and life in the unwholesome garret, the damp prison, the pestilential hospital, the long vigil of some sick saint's bedside, who perhaps could not afford a nurse to watch her? How often have you given up a pleasant evening with your family to carry comfort or salvation to some other soul? How often have you denied yourself some gratification or necessity that you might have something to give to Christ to send the gospel to the perishing? These are the only badges of honor and reward in the kingdom of God. Service is only duty. When we have done all "we are unworthy servants; we have only done our duty" (Luke 17:10). It is only the crimson blood of sacrifice that can make us partakers of the sufferings and glory of our Lord.

3. Epaphroditus possessed the spirit of silence and self-forgetfulness in service and suffering.

Most people want their sacrifices known and the story of their service told in the glowing records of human praise. Their chief sorrow is the sense of the world's neglect and want of sympathy. But here is a man whose only desire is to keep his friends from knowing of his troubles, and whose only heaviness was because they "heard he was ill" (Philippians 2:26). So unselfish and considerate was he that he only desired to spare them the news that might bring anxiety and concern. This is very fine. It touches the deepest lines of love and Christlikeness. It is the veil of humility and the covering of unselfishness which adds to sacrifice and service a divine touch and claims for it a heavenly reward. The things we do to be seen by men—the things that others appreciate, pity, praise—of these the Master says: "[t]hey have received their reward" (Matthew 6:16). But the things done only unto Him, and forgotten perhaps by us as soon as done, or esteemed as of small account because it was merely second nature for us to do them, of these He says, "[y]our Father, who sees what is done in secret, will reward you" (6:18).

The happy souls who are to sit at the right hand of the King when He comes in the glory of His Father, and hear Him say, "Come, you who are blessed by my Father; take your inheritance, the kingdom prepared for you since the creation of the world. For I was hungry and you gave me something to eat, I was thirsty and you gave me something to drink" (25:34–35), will have forgotten all about their service and will answer, "Lord, when did we see you hungry and feed you, or thirsty and give you something to drink" (25:37)? But their very self-unconsciousness will but add to the value of their service, and the greatness of their reward in the day when He shall "bring to light what is hidden in darkness and will expose the motives of men's hearts. At that time each will receive his praise from God" (1 Corinthians 4:5).

Lessons for Us

Now the qualities we have been describing are among the finest touches of character. One may be a sincere Christian, and an irreproachable and righteous man, and not possess them. Yes, but it is these fine qualities that constitute the difference between the boor and the gentleman, between the piece of charcoal and the diamond, between the sunflower and the rose, between the soul saved "as one escaping through the flames" (1 Corinthians 3:15), and the glorified saint sweeping through the gates with an abundant entrance "into the eternal kingdom of our Lord and Savior Jesus Christ" (2 Peter 1:11).

And it is not infrequently that a great issue is decided by what seems a trifling incident, but what really indicates some high quality beneath. The fact that 300 of Gideon's 10,000 men lapped up the water when they drank, showed that they alone possessed the qualities that could be depended upon in the crisis hour. The fact that the widow of Zarephath was willing to give up her last handful of meal and her last drop of oil, marked in her spirit a quality which prepared her in later years to receive back her boy as the first to rise from the dead. The readiness of Abraham to give up his only son at God's command was but a straw on the tide of his life, but it showed the bent and purpose of his being, and God could say, "Now I know that you fear God" (Genesis 22:12). The simple incident in Daniel's history when he refused the royal dainties and stuck to his simple fare, was an index to his entire character and demonstrated the fixed purpose, the inflexible principle, and the self-denying simplicity of the man whom God could depend upon in any test.

These may seem trifles, "but trifles make perfection, and perfection is no trifle." These may not be among "whatever is true and whatever is pure" (Philippians 4:8), but they are among "whatever is lovely" (4:8). And God wants us to be arrayed "in the splendor of his holiness" (Psalms 96:9), as well as "a robe of righteousness" (Isaiah 61:10). It is this that constitutes the difference between the justified and the sanctified, the clean robe and the marriage robe, the mere forgiveness of our sins and the great reward of him who overcomes.

God is giving us all along the way the opportunity of winning these victories, of putting on these wedding robes, of gaining these great rewards. Let us not miss the opportunity; let us not despise the proffered prize.

The soldiers of England and America have counted it the chance of a lifetime to be called to the post of danger and the opportunity of swift promotion. This is the way the heroes of Santiago, Manila, Dhargai and Glencoe, have looked upon their hardships and their dangers. And the verdict of history has already been pronounced, that, so far as earthly fame is worth contending for, they have not counted amiss or suffered in vain. And shall we who strive for a better crown think less of the promised prize, or complain when the trials come, through which we are permitted to win it? Shall we not rather meet every situation with holy and jealous care? Forge our future crowns out of our fiery trials? Turn opposition, temptation and suffering into occasions for putting on more fully all the graces of the Spirit and all the strength of Christ? So that at last we shall stand perfect and complete in all the will of God, with that happy company of whom it shall be said: " 'For the wedding of the Lamb has come,/ and his bride has made herself ready/ Fine linen, bright and clean,/ was given her to wear.' (Fine linen stands for the righteous acts of the saints.)" (Revelation 19:7). "They follow the Lamb wherever he goes. . . . No lie was found in their mouths; they are blameless" (14:4–5).

CHAPTER 4

The Christian Temper, Supernatural and Divine

I want to know Christ and the power of his resurrection and the fellowship of sharing in his sufferings, becoming like him in his death, and so, somehow, to attain to the resurrection from the dead. (Philippians 3:10–11)

The temper of which we have been speaking is not natural but supernatural. This delicate plant is not indigenous to the soil of time, but must be transplanted from heavenly soil and grow from a supernatural seed. We talk about innocent babies, angelic maidens and lovely dispositions, but these things all disappear when the real test comes, and we find ourselves like one sitting down on a beautiful mossy bank covered with verdure and bloom, and suddenly seeing the poisonous asp glide from beneath our seat. The life described in this heavenly picture must come from a heavenly source, and is possible only after the natural has died out and the resurrection life of Christ has taken its place.

In our text the apostle describes by a reference to his own experience the evolution of the Christian temper.

1. A Natural Virtue

There is such a thing as natural virtue. There are moral differences in human nature, and God does not disparage or deprecate whatever goodness still remains after the wreck of the fall. Paul acknowledges that even he had been possessed of many qualities of virtue and morality. If any man had cause to have confidence in himself, surely he had. He gives a list of his virtues, and moral and religious advantages. He was strictly orthodox, born of Hebrew blood, circumcised according to the rigid ritual of Judaism, a "Hebrew of the Hebrews," a Pharisee of the Pharisees, blameless so far as outward righteousness was concerned, and intensely earnest so far as religious zeal could go. Yet all this he renounces and disclaims with one emphatic sentence, "But whatever was to my profit I now consider loss for the sake of Christ" (Philippians 3:7).

2. Renounce Our Own Righteousness

In order to receive the righteousness of Christ we must renounce all our own righteousness. The surrender which Christianity demands is not the abandoning of evil, but the renouncing of even that which is good for the sake of God's better and best. All his own righteousness and all his own rights Paul gladly surrendered. He had counted them loss. He had suffered their loss and then he had not allowed one lingering regret, one reluctant thought, but counted them all refuse, not worthy to speak about in comparison with the excellence of the knowledge and the glory of the righteousness of his precious Lord. He had accepted a new righteousness by faith from Christ, and it was all divine. He does not mean by this merely his justification from past sin through the imputed righteousness of Christ; but he means that he had accepted from his Lord an interior, intrinsic and personal righteousness, that his inward character and whole nature henceforth were not the result of self-culture but the infusion of the very life and spirit of his blessed Master.

3. *A Deeper Place of Surrender*

There is a deeper place of surrender than the renunciation of our righteousness. "I want to know Christ . . . and the fellowship of sharing in his sufferings" (3:10). Merely to die to our sinfulness or our righteousness is but a preliminary of holy character. The essence of it is to enter into the most profound and perfect union with the Lord Jesus even to the extent of longing to be made partakers of His very sufferings.

I once knew a Christian friend who offered this singular prayer for a loved one, and I know nothing that ever impressed me more. "Lord," she said, "I ask Thee that Thou wilt lay on me all the burdens, sufferings, trials and needs of my friend. I do not ask to share the joys, but I do ask if there be pain, pressure, danger, that I can bear, to lay it upon me in sympathy, fellowship, prayer, and the power to lift and help so that the life for which I suffer may be the more free to serve and work for Thee."

Love always longs to bear another's pain, and so the heart of the apostle intensely longed to share the sufferings of Christ. There is a sense in which this may be done if we live near enough to His heart.

There are some sufferings which we cannot call the sufferings of Christ. They are our own. The sufferings which we bring upon ourselves by sin or folly we have no right to call His sufferings. The sufferings that come to us even through sickness we may lay on Him, for He has already borne them, and He does not ask us to bear them again if we are walking in His will and trusting in His Word. The reproaches and persecutions, as we call them, which we bring upon ourselves by indiscretion or wrongdoing, these are not the sufferings of Christ, although He lovingly helps us in the trials which we needlessly endure.

Then He had sufferings which we cannot share. His vicarious suffering as our Substitute and Sacrifice for sin, we can never endure and never need to. Once for all He has appeared to "do away with sin by the sacrifice of himself" (Hebrews 9:26), and "no sacrifice for sins is left" (10:26).

But there are sufferings which we may share with Him. There was His voluntary self-sacrifice for the world's salvation into which we may enter as we give ourselves for others and sacrifice the pleasures of the world that we may walk with Him. There is again the misunderstanding and loneliness, persecution and distress which will come to all who live godly in Christ Jesus in every age, and which we may joyfully accept, counting it a privilege that we are esteemed worthy to suffer for the name of Jesus. And deeper than all, there is the spirit of sympathy with the suffering around us, the tempted and tried, the sorrows and even the sins of a lost world. This is the deepest element in the priesthood of Christ which His disciples may share. "For we do not have a high priest who is unable to sympathize with our weaknesses" (4:15). The Christlike life will enter with Him into His deep sense of the needs of others, into the ministry of prayer and agony for the sins and sorrows of men and into His deepest thoughts and tenderest solicitude for the lost world. Paul tells us in his epistles of the burdens, care and griefs that came upon him constantly for the cause of His Master and the condition of his brethren.

Now in his letter to the Colossians he tells us, "Now I rejoice in what was suffered for you, and I fill up in my flesh what is still lacking in regard to Christ's afflictions, for the sake of his body, which is the church" (1:24). That is to say, Christ has left certain sufferings for His body, the Church, to finish, and Paul rejoiced in being partaker of these sufferings. Writing to the Philippians he says of this very thing, "But even if I am being poured out like a drink offering on the sacrifice and service coming from your faith, I am glad and rejoice with all of you. So you too should be glad and rejoice with me" (2:17). It was his joy and glory to be a living sacrifice for his beloved brethren, and he expected them to respond in the same spirit, "Carry each other's burdens, and in this way you will fulfill the law of Christ" (Galatians 6:2). And accordingly in one of his letters to the Corinthians, he exclaims, "Who is weak, and I do not feel weak? Who is led into sin, and I do not inwardly burn? Besides everything else, I face daily the pressure of my concern for all the churches" (2 Corinthians 11:29, 28).

4. Becoming Like Him in His Death

There is one step more, "becoming like him in his death" (Philippians 3:10). The difference between suffering and death is that there is no suffering after death. The dead man is one whom the suffering has ceased to hurt, and when we are truly conformable unto Christ's death, we are in that happy place where the promise of Jeremiah is true, "It does not fear when heat comes;/ . . . It has no worries in a year of drought/ and never fails to bear fruit" (Jeremiah 17:8). The people that are always talking about their deadness are not yet dead. The people who are fond of dwelling on their sufferings have not yet become like Him in His death. To be dead with Christ is to be as if we were not, and to so recognize ourselves in Him that we shall not know our old selves, and shall even think and speak of ourselves as Paul when he said, "I [knew] a man in Christ . . . fourteen years ago" (2 Corinthians 12:2). It was as if it were another, and not himself. It is not to die with Christ that the apostle is speaking of, but it is to *be dead* with Christ. This everlasting dying is not deadness, but it is aliveness. Many are like the cowardly Nero, who when pursued by his enemies, stabbed himself in a score of places, but was careful every time to avoid a fatal part. The place of victory and rest is where we are really dead, and so dead that we have even ceased to be conscious of it, and are conscious only of Christ and the resurrection life which has come to us through Him.

5. *Spiritual Resurrection*

But now we come to something far more important than this, namely, the spiritual resurrection by which we are able to enter into the sufferings and death of our Lord. Now this whole passage is a perfect paradox, and runs directly contrary to the natural order of logical thought. In such an order we would expect the death to come first and the resurrection afterwards, but here it is quite different. It is "the power of his resurrection" first, then the "fellowship of his sufferings" and the conformity to His death. The explanation of this leads us to the deepest spiritual truths. We can never truly suffer or die with Christ by mere willpower or in stern, cold, dead surrender. We can never do it truly until we have first entered into His life, and are enabled for it by the power of life, hope and love. The reason the Lord Jesus was able to stoop to the very grave and lay down all His rights and honors was because He had so much above and beyond all this in His Father's love and His own eternal glory, that the sacrifice and surrender could not really harm or impoverish Him. His life was not in the things He laid down, but in the things He could not lose; and it was for the joy set before Him that He endured the cross, scorning the shame (Hebrews 12:2). The power of an endless life was filling all His being and gave Him strength to make the mighty sacrifice and go down among the dead, because just before Him He saw the brightness of the resurrection, the glory of the ascension and the kingdom of the coming age. And so His people must know the power of His resurrection and the fellowship of His glory, before they can in any true spirit enter into the fellowship of His sufferings and the partnership of His death.

How was it that the patriarch Abraham was able to sacrifice on the altar of Moriah him in whom all his hopes, as well as affections, were bound up, and with whom all the promises of God's covenant were inseparably connected? It was only because of the power of His resurrection which Abraham had already felt and seen. In commenting on this scene the apostle explains to the Hebrews that he esteemed that "Abraham reasoned that God could raise the dead, and figuratively speaking, he did receive Isaac back from death" (11:19). This makes it certain that Abraham confidently expected Isaac's resurrection before he offered him up to death.

We can see this plainly even in the Old Testament narrative, when he said to the attendants, "Stay here with the donkey while I and the boy go over there. We will worship and then we will come back to you" (Genesis 22:5). He certainly expected to return with Isaac, and it was this blessed hope and this triumphant faith that took the sting from his sorrow and gave life and victory to his awful sacrifice.

And so we must have the spring of divine joy and victorious faith before we can stoop to a true surrender. It is not yielding to blind fate; it is not giving up in dark despair. It is simply entering the dark tunnel, knowing that the light of home is on the farther side, and that we have a hope and a certainty which even death itself cannot destroy.

Indeed, beloved friends, we cannot yield in anything acceptably to God, unless we have the life and strength of God within us to make it possible and real. We are not even able to consecrate ourselves in our own strength. We must take His life for all, even for the surrender, and through the power of His resurrection enter into His death and share the fellowship of His sufferings. This takes the spirit of asceticism out of Christian life, and crowns our very sacrifice with all the joy and the glory of victorious faith. It is faith that works by love and overcomes the world and even the grave.

Be assured, beloved brethren, that this is the deepest secret of spiritual life. There is no merit in enforced suffering or unwilling sacrifice. God asks no sacrifice from you until it is such joy that it has ceased to be a sacrifice. He wants no tears of reluctance on His altar; but He wants our hearts to come with willing, joyful yieldedness, and count it a privilege and honor that He will condescend to take us, own us, and make the best of our worthless lives. The spirit of the New Testament is this, radiant and bright with the light of love and promise.

> Therefore, I urge you, brothers, in view of God's mercy, to offer your bodies as living sacrifices, holy and pleasing to God— this is your spiritual act of worship. Do not conform any longer to the pattern of this world, but be transformed by the renewing of your mind. Then you will be able to test and approve what God's will is—his good, pleasing, and perfect will. (Romans 12:1–2)

6. The Light of Hope

Once more, we have not only the light of faith, but the still more radiant light of hope, as the inspiration of this glad surrender: "and so, somehow, to attain to the resurrection from the dead" (Philippians 3:11). There can be no doubt about the application of this passage to the resurrection of God's prepared people, who are to rise and meet the Bridegroom at His glorious coming. It is not a general resurrection of all the dead, but it is a select resurrection and an elect company who are taken from among the rest of the dead. It is the resurrection described in the 20th chapter of Revelation where the crowned ones come forth to sit on the millennial throne with their regent Lord,

> (The rest of the dead did not come to life until the thousand years were ended.) This is the first resurrection. Blessed and holy are those who have part in the first resurrection. The second death has no power over them, but they will be priests of God and of Christ and will reign with him for a thousand years. (Revelation 20:5–6)

This was the hope which inspired the apostle to let all else go, and rise in the present life to the highest and holiest possibilities of Christian experience and communion with his Lord. For this he counted all but loss, and said he was still striving for something unto which he had not yet fully attained. It is very solemn to hear this extraordinary man, even at this ripe stage of his life, speaking of the blessed hope of the first resurrection as something to which he had not yet surely attained. Later, in his second letter to Timothy, it is different. He speaks of it there as a crown that is laid up for him, a fight that is fought, a race that is run, a course that is finished, and a prize that is sure. But in this chapter he is still pressing on to gain it, and it is the inspiration of his glorious career. Shall it be the inspiration of our lives?

Is it not true even in the nature of things that our inward character takes on its appropriate outward form? It is part of the law of the fitness of things that the coarse and groveling nature of the swine should be embodied in the gross form of the hog; that the deep and subtle, cunning serpent should take shape in the slimy, crawling reptile; and that the gentleness of the dove should be expressed in its downy bosom and its gentle, lovely form. Do we not see this in human character? Do we not find character expressing itself in the personal appearance? Does not the criminal become stereotyped with the lines of cruelty, hardness and coarseness in his very visage? Does not purity, gentleness and nobility stamp its effect on the brow of the good and cover the sweet face of some aged saint with a beauty and glory that shine from the sacred Holy of holies within? Have we not all looked upon faces that were an absolute reflection of the transparent life that we knew was there behind the lovely countenance, and have we not looked upon countenances that were but the outward photograph of the dark, deep, dreadful hell that was raging in the heart beneath? And if this be in so great a measure true in this imperfect state, how much more will it be realized in that world where the law of the fitness of things shall be absolute and eternal. There Judas shall not only find his own place, but be clothed with his own form. There the wicked shall come creeping forth from their dark tombs with all the meanness, malignity and terror of their past lives and their future doom expressed in their terrific personality. And there the holy and the good shall rise with every feature beaming, and every movement telling of the gladness within and the glory that is to come.

Yes, we are forging our crowns day by day. We are weaving our triumphal robes. We are making our eternal destiny. We are settling into our final place. And the glory which the Master is preparing for each of us, He is working into us now in the firstfruits of the Spirit, who is "a deposit guaranteeing our inheritance until the redemption of those who are God's possession" (Ephesians 1:14).

"Grant," cried the mother of two disciples, "that one of these two sons of mine may sit at your right and the other at your left in your kingdom" (Matthew 20:21). The Master did not refuse her behest, but He told them very solemnly that it was largely in their own hands, and that these places of honor were to be given by the Father to those for whom they were prepared. He also showed very plainly what this preparation meant by the question: "Can you drink the cup I am going to drink" (20:22)? Thus alone could they enter into His glory, "If we died with him,/ we will also live with him;/ if we endure,/ we will also reign with him" (2 Timothy 2:11–12).

CHAPTER 5

The Christian Temper, Aggressive and Progressive

Not that I have already obtained all this, or have already been made perfect, but I press on to take hold of that for which Christ Jesus took hold of me. Brothers, I do not consider myself yet to have taken hold of it. But one thing I do: Forgetting what is behind and straining toward what is ahead, I press on toward the goal to win the prize for which God has called me heavenward in Christ Jesus. (Philippians 3:12–14)

It might be supposed that a spirit of sweetness would necessarily be a spirit of weakness, and that a yielded and gentle disposition is lacking in the spirit of forceful aggressiveness and manly energy. This is not always true. The bravest soldier is often the gentlest man. The quiet forces of nature are the most irresistible and overwhelming, and the strength of God is often hidden behind His gentleness.

And so this passage proves that the man who

could be most yielding, tender and affectionate, could stand adamant or sweep like the cyclone. This fine passage has about it something that reminds us of the clarion call of the trumpet summoning to arms and to victory, something that suggests the atmosphere of the arena where men struggle for the mastery and where crowns are dearly won.

The spirit of our age is marked by physical culture. Our young people are taught in schools, universities and colleges to train for athletic skill and physical strength. This is perhaps carried to an extreme degree as it was in the luxurious days of ancient Rome which preceded the final catastrophe. At least, it expresses a longing in the soul for manly energy, and may well stimulate us to the higher pursuit of spiritual manhood and aggressive forcefulness. If the flower of our manhood is contending in the athletic arena or on the field of battle for the prizes of victory, how much more should we strive for a crown that is incorruptible and a glory which does not fade?

This is the picture of our text. It is the spectacle of a man pressing forward in the racecourse with muscles strained to their utmost tension, with nerves alert and senses all alive to every advantage of the fray, and with his whole being intensely absorbed in the struggle for a prize which is flashing before his kindling eye from the open heavens where the great Umpire stands beckoning him on and holding out the glorious diadem.

There are three important features in the picture, full of precious lessons for us who with him are also in the race.

A Spirit of Self-Dissatisfaction

"Not that I have already obtained all this, or have already been made perfect, . . . I do not consider myself yet to have taken hold of it" (3:12–13). There is nothing that so deadens the spiritual activities and aspirations as an overwhelming self-complacency. If we look at mere human standards, or even our own ideals, we shall easily be satisfied. The story of the artist who turned away from his perfect and finished workmanship with a cry of despair, "I have surpassed myself; henceforth there is nothing left for my ambition," is a true glimpse of the paralyzing power of a too-easy self-content. It needs the sense of our own shortcomings to incite us to nobler endeavors. There is a discouraging way of looking at your faults and failures which takes all the heart out of you. But there is a wholesome mean between conceit and self-condemnation which is the fruitful soil of new endeavor and loftier aspiration.

In two respects Paul felt that he had up to this time failed to reach the full ideal. First, he had not yet obtained the prize or made sure of it. This word translated *attained* (KJV) ought to be rendered *obtained* [which the modern NIV uses]. He is not referring to character but to reward. A little later he felt he had secured it, and in writing to Timothy he could say, "I have fought the good fight, I have finished the race, I have kept the faith. Now there is in store for me the crown of righteousness" (2 Timothy 4:7).

Next, however, he adds, "or have already been made perfect" (Philippians 3:12). This should be translated "perfected," and it refers to personal character and attainment. What then does the apostle mean when later in the paragraph he adds, "All of us who are mature [perfect, KJV] should take such a view of things" (3:15)? How can he be perfect if he is not yet perfect? The answer will be plain if we paraphrase his statement in a very simple form. We are perfect but not perfected. We are complete but not completed. "And you have been given fullness [are complete, KJV] in Christ" (Colossians 2:10), says the apostle to the Colossians, and yet in the same epistle he adds, "that you may stand firm in all the will of God, mature and fully assured [perfect and complete, KJV]" (4:12). There is a sense, a true sense in which we may accept the righteousness and grace of the Lord Jesus Christ and count it real and sufficient, and dare to say, "He is made unto me sanctification," and "I am complete in Him." As far as our faith goes, as far as our light goes, we are fully saved. We are all there in Christ just as fully as the newborn baby is complete in all its parts. But it is not yet full-grown. It has all the organs its father has, but they are yet immature. It is complete but not completed. It is perfect but not perfected. And so the consecrated soul that has taken Christ in His fullness has Him in His fullness, but yet there is to be a deeper revelation and larger fullness step by step and day by day, until at last he shall reach the "whole measure of the fullness of Christ" (Ephesians 4:13).

Do not let us, therefore, depreciate ourselves too much or fail to recognize our glorious standing and our heavenly place in Christ Jesus our Lord. But do not let us, at the same time, forget how much there still remains to be possessed, and standing midway between the confidence of faith and the aspiration of hope, let us press on from strength to strength, from faith to faith, from grace to glory.

A Spirit Of Heavenly Aspiration And Holy Aggressiveness

Along with this sense of shortcoming there comes to the apostle the deep, intense desire to press on to all that yet remains in his inheritance of grace. The picture is an intense one. It flashes with the light of the arena; it rings with the bugle notes of battle and triumph. It sweeps on with the celerity of the cavalry charge and the triumphal march. There is something about its phrases that stirs our very hearts, and makes every drop of blood to throb with strange intensity. It is a soul in earnest. It is a heart aflame. It is a life all aglow with divine enthusiasm and superhuman strength. It is no soft sentimentalism, but it is spiritual manhood in the glory of its mightiest strength. It is the athlete in the arena. It is the conqueror on the field of victory.

1. Forgetting the Past

"Forgetting what is behind" (Philippians 3:13). There is much behind and it is not to be despised, but it is not to be a pillow of soft and indolent repose to stifle and satisfy our higher ambition. Compared with all that is yet before us it is only a foundation. And the larger that foundation is the mightier must be the superstructure that is to crown it. Suppose that you were to point me to a massive pile of brick and stone on some splendid site no higher than the foundation walls of some great building, and tell me with exultant pride of the deep excavations, the costly carvings and the splendid building you had erected. I would laugh in your face as I looked at the cellars flooded with the storm, the walls crumbling under the destroying elements, the rubbish accumulating on the terraces, and the very creatures of the wilderness finding a lair and hiding place amid the rubbish. I would say to you, "The very grandeur of your foundation calls for a still grander superstructure. It is ridiculous for you to boast of what you have already done until these walls have been reared at least a dozen stories higher, and the roof has enclosed these spaces and the chambers are divided and adorned in a manner worthy of your costly beginnings." And so the more God has done for you already, the more need there is that you should look well to it, "that you do not lose what you have worked for, but that you may be rewarded fully" (2 John 8).

2. *A Right Concept of the Future*

"Straining toward what is ahead" (Philippians 3:13). Man differs from the lower orders of creation in this, that while like them his past is limited by the little space of time since his existence, unlike them his future is unlimited; his lifetime is eternity. He is endowed with the divine gift of an immortal future. He has the ages upon ages yet to come in which to expand and develop forevermore.

When Alexander the Great divided his old dominion among his faithful followers, he kept nothing for himself. They asked him in surprise about his portion. "What have you kept for yourself?" they said, and he pointed into the distance and simply said, "Hope." The future was his inheritance, and before many months had passed that future had brought him an empire vaster than all he had given away, and mightier than the world ever knew.

And so God is teaching us to live in the imperial realm of hope. There are souls who have no eyes for the future. They cannot see over the heads of the things that immediately surround them. They live in the present, and they are baffled by their immediate difficulties, toils and troubles. Life for them is enclosed by the boundaries of the setting sun. But there are other souls who see into life's tomorrow, and over the head of difficulty, disaster and even death itself. They see evermore the eternal morning, and they sing, "it is better farther on." The things that are not are to them more real than the things that are. Faith and hope create a world yet unrevealed and yet most real, which satisfies and stimulates their triumphant spirits as they press on to the things that are before.

Beloved, ask God to give you a sanctified imagination, a quickened vision of the unseen, a power to see what others cannot see, and to hear what others do not hear. May He put eternity in your heart and make your life as large as the immeasurable years on which God has projected the orbit of your being.

3. Following After

Having turned from the past and caught the vision of the future he now presses on to meet it. The figure is that of the hunter pursuing the coveted game. There is a strange fascination in this. Men will follow a trail for days and weeks to get a single moose up in the woods of Maine, and after exposure, toil and suffering will feel amply repaid by a single specimen of the splendid quarry. Mile after mile the snow-covered forest is traversed over windfalls, morasses, pitfalls and perils which they would not think of encountering in the sober business of life. But it is nothing to them as they pursue their prey with a fascination that takes away all sense of toil or computation of time. So, when God has given the glowing vision of His highest will, nothing is hard or long in its attainment. Step by step through toil and trial the soul presses on for the crown incorruptible and the heavenly goal.

Beloved, are you as much in earnest about the best things as you are for your pleasures, recreations or your earthly gain? Let this lofty standard measure our individual lives.

4. *Pressing Toward the Goal*

"I press on toward the goal" (Philippians 3:14). The language is intense. It is the expression of the most profound earnestness of which a human soul is capable. It is no child's play. It is no sentimental dream. It is no incidental mood. It is no mere occasional fit of transient enthusiasm. It is the habit of the life. It is the sweep of the volcano down the mountain side which carries everything in its course and transforms everything into its fiery torrent. Beloved, it is a life in earnest. Is it yours?

5. *Singleness of Purpose*

Singleness of purpose is the secret of this successful and intensely earnest life. "But one thing I do" (3:13). The grandeur of his great purpose eclipses all other aims and excludes all competing interests. Our life is too short and too small to be scattered in a dozen directions. We can be our best only as we let God compact us and press us with all His power and all the strenuousness of our strength in one direction, and that, of course, the highest and the best. Beloved, is this the single purpose of your life? You have but one life. God help you to give it all to Him and gain it all from Him in its glorious outcome.

The Divine Cooperation

There is more than the figure of the spiritual

athlete pressing on for the prize. There is another Form in this picture that is standing behind him and helping him on. Or, to change the metaphor, the glorious Umpire at the heavenly goal is not an indifferent spectator, coolly waiting to give the crowns to the conquering ones without any personal interest as to who shall overcome. No, He is an interested partner in the race. He is bending from His throne and beckoning to the racer as he runs, and with encouraging smile and gesture of inspiration is calling to him: "Be of good cheer, press on. You will overcome. I am holding your hand as well as holding out your crown. I have overcome for you and you will overcome through Me." This is the finest part of the picture. Paul is not alone with his struggle; his Master is with him, and he is only apprehending that for which he has been also apprehended of Christ Jesus (3:12, KJV).

In three respects Christ cooperates with His people's heavenly aspirations.

1. He reveals the vision and the prize.

It is He who reveals the vision of the glory and the prize. A little later in the passage we read, "All of us who are mature should take such a view of things. And if on some point you think differently, that too God will make clear to you" (3:15). Perhaps this glowing picture has not appealed to all your hearts. Perhaps there are some simple commonplace lives who have said, "I have no imagination, I have no opportunity for these glorious things. My task is one of lowly toil and ceaseless drudgery. I try to do my duty as best I can, but I don't understand the exalted feelings of which you have been telling me. This is not for me."

Beloved, "And if on some point you think differently, that too God will make clear to you" (3:15).

There was a time when it was nothing to Paul but a light in his heart above the brightness of the sunshine. Then God revealed to him another world of reality, and gave him the spiritual senses to discern it and dwell in it. The same revelation will come to you if you humbly ask and wait for it.

A lady in London once called upon Dr. Boardman and complained to him that she had no spiritual feeling. The good doctor turned to Ephesians 3:20: "Now to him who is able to do immeasurably more than all we ask or imagine." He told her to go home and pray over that one verse until God made it fully real to her, and then come back and tell him when her experience measured up to it. She went away and continued for many days to pray that one prayer, not expecting much from it at first. But one day she came back to see the good minister. With eyes moist with tears and lips trembling with holy gladness, she told him that no language could describe, no prayer could express, no thought could compass, the unutterable fullness of joy which the Holy Spirit had poured into her heart. God had revealed even this to her.

I had a brother once on earth, now in heaven, who was very rigid and conservative in his ideas of religious experience. He looked upon all demonstrations of feeling as sentimental and unscriptural. He was much disgusted with many of the manifestations of spiritual power and earnestness connected with the early days of our own work. At length his health broke down, and he was manifestly drawing near to a great crisis. I endeavored in vain to bring him to that place of tender spiritual feeling where he could take Christ as his Healer or even as his Comforter. But it only met with recoil. Then the case was committed to God in believing prayer; and he waited. One day several months later, a letter came from that brother telling of a marvelous change. The day before while reading a verse in his Bible, a flood of light had burst in to his soul, and for hours he could only praise and pray and wonder. Yes, he, too, had become a fanatic, if this were fanaticism, and God had done exceeding abundantly above all that he could ask or think. His cold intellectual nature was submerged in a baptism of love which never ceased to pour its fullness through his being, until a few weeks later he swept through the gates of glory shouting the praises of his Redeemer.

Beloved, would you have the vision? "And if on some point you think differently, that too God will make clear to you" (Philippians 3:15).

2. *He calls us to the prize.*

"Of the high calling of God in Christ Jesus" (3:14, KJV), is translated better in the revised version, "the upward calling," or, better still in another version, "the prize to which he has called us from on high." God called Abraham in Mesopotamia, and he left all and followed. He called Moses in the desert, and he gave up everything to obey. He called Elisha from his plow, and he quickly responded. He called the disciples from their fishing nets, and they went with the Master. He called Paul, and he was "not disobedient unto the heavenly vision" (Acts 26:19, KJV). Beloved, He is calling you. Do not miss the call and the crown.

3. *He holds our hand.*

He is holding the hand of the competitor for the prize, and upholding him in the conflict. This expression, "obtained," literally means "grasped," and the apostle says that he is grasping that for which Christ has grasped him. There is a hand underneath. There is a power behind. There is a loving pressure that will not let him go. God loves us better than we love ourselves. In spite of ourselves, He is saving us to the uttermost and carrying us through to the fullness of His uttermost salvation. We are not alone. He will not let us fail.

CHAPTER 6

A Spirit of Love, Joy and Peace

I plead with Euodia and I plead with Syntyche to agree with each other in the Lord. . . .

Rejoice in the Lord always. I will say it again: Rejoice! Let your gentleness be evident to all. The Lord is near. Do not be anxious about anything, but in everything, by prayer and petition, with thanksgiving, present your requests to God. (Philippians 4:2, 4–6)

This passage reaches the very heart of the sweetest Christian life. It combines the four choicest ingredients of the fruit of the Spirit, namely: love, joy, peace and sweetness.

Love

The first is love. There are three kinds of love unfolded in these verses. The first is Paul's love to his friends and flock. How tenderly he addresses them: "[my] brothers" (3:1), he says, associating himself with them in the heavenly ties of the divine family. "[y]ou whom I love" (4:1), he adds, mingling with this holy relationship all the tenderness of human affection. And "long for" (4:1). This is more than tenderness. This is the affection that dwells continually on the beloved object, wearies of his absence and longs for fellowship and reunion. "My joy" (4:1), a still stronger expression of the dependence of his very happiness upon their fellowship and love. "And crown"(4:1), this carries forward the bonds of love and friendship to the eternal sphere, and links all his eternal hopes and rewards with his dearly beloved friends at Philippi. It was thus that the early Christians loved one another, and it is still true that "everyone who loves the father loves his child as well" (1 John 5:1).

Next, we have a reference to their mutual love of one another. Among the saints at Philippi were two sisters whose names signify "success" and "fame." They were evidently valued workers in the church, but, like many good women, they were not able to agree with each other in the same mind and judgment. Each was a woman of such strong character and individuality and such excellent common sense and judgment that she could not see how she could be wrong in her view of the matter, and her sister be right; and so they were frequently at variance, and their misunderstandings were evidently hurting the little flock. Paul does not reprove them or even enjoin them, but he gets down on his knees to one of them and asks his friend Epaphroditus to do the same with the other, and they just beseech them to "agree with each other in the Lord" (Philippians 4:2). This is very touching and humbling to us in our misunderstandings and strifes. Thus the Master is beseeching us to be of one mind and one spirit in the Lord.

But the best of all is that the apostle gives us here the secret of attaining to oneness of spirit, a thing not so easily done with strong and independent minds, especially when each is sure she is right. The secret is this, "in the Lord." Don't try to bring your sister to your mind. Don't try to come to her mind, but let each of you drop her own opinion and preference and move out of yourselves into the Lord, and agree jointly and severally to take His thought about it whatever it may be, and even before you know it. And you will always find that His mind about everything is one that does justice to both parties, and lifts both to a higher plane where they can be fully one.

At the same time the apostle entreats his friend to help them both, and he very distinctly tells him of their value and importance; for it is of them he speaks when he says they "contended at my side in the cause of the gospel" (4:3), and "whose names are in the book of life" (4:3).

Then there is a third expression of love in the little phrase which he addresses to his own fellow laborer, "loyal yokefellow" (4:3). This tells not only of Paul's love to his friends but of their love to him. It is a beautiful figure and speaks of perfect fellowship and mutual service and suffering. The Lord Himself uses the same figure respecting His fellowship with us when He says: "Take my yoke upon you and learn from me, for I am gentle and humble in heart" (Matthew 11:29). How beautiful and blessed if we might be to each other as true yokefellows as our blessed and heavenly Friend has been to us!

Joy

Here again we have the same little talisman which tells the secret of the heavenly life, "in the Lord." We may not be able to rejoice in circumstances, feelings or even friends, but we can still rejoice in the Lord. This is the heavenly element of our joy. It comes entirely from sources beyond our own nature or surroundings, and it often contradicts every rational consideration and makes us wonder even at our own joy. It is the joy of Christ throbbing in the heart where He dwells. It was of this He spoke when He said, "I have told you this so that my joy may be in you and that your joy may be complete" (John 15:11).

Again, it is a constant, uninterrupted and unlimited joy. "Rejoice in the Lord always" (Philippians 4:4). There is positively no situation where we should cease to rejoice; no reason that could justify us in discouragement or depression. It is the normal, uniform and unvarying temper of the Christian life. "Your sun will never set again,/ and your moon will wane no more;/ the LORD will be your everlasting light,/ and your days of sorrow will end" (Isaiah 60:20). If the fig tree does not blossom, and the fruit is not upon the vine, we must still "rejoice in the LORD,/ . . . [and] be joyful in God my Savior" (Habakkuk 3:18).

If the dearest friends disappoint us or leave us, the Lord remains, and we must not cease our singing. If our own feelings even betray us, and our hearts seem dead and cold, still we must "Consider it pure joy" (James 1:2), though we do not feel it, and take by faith the gladness that we do not find in our own consciousness. And if trials roll over us like surging waves and raging billows, we must raise the keynote higher, and exchanging joy for triumph, we must "glory in tribulation also" (Romans 5:3, KJV).

Once more, this joy is persistent and refuses to be defeated or discouraged, for he repeats the command with strange insistence, and as though he were speaking against some barrier of difficulty, some cloud of discouragement, some weight of deep depression; "again," he adds, "I say rejoice" (Philippians 4:4). It is a redoubled command. It has a twofold significance, and whatever else we fail to do we must rejoice.

Now, dear friends, we do not say this is the uniform experience of the children of God. We are simply pointing out in this epistle the rarer and choicer qualities of the Christian temper. It is the ideal character if it is not always the real, and as we pursue the ideal and refuse to take lower ground, God will make it real. Do not, therefore, be discouraged if you have sometimes failed to reach this lofty and settled standard, and to dwell on high in this lofty poise of victorious gladness; but take it as your ideal, pursue it as your goal, claim it as your privilege. Remember that sadness, discouragement, depression, are always of the enemy and must surely weaken your faith, your love, your holiness, your usefulness, your healing, your prayers, your whole Christian life. Therefore, "Rejoice in the Lord always. I will say it again: Rejoice!" (4:4).

Sweetness of Spirit

"Let your gentleness be evident to all" (4:5). The Greek word translated "gentleness" is difficult to turn into English, but the various meanings that have been given to it are all suggestive and helpful, and each has certain degrees of truth in it. The first of these is the Authorized Version, "moderation." This is the temperate spirit, the disciplined heart, the self-control which comes to a well-ordered mind, the quietness, sense and moderation which keep us from all extremes, and hold us in the golden mean of a sound mind.

Again, it has been translated "yieldedness." This is also a valuable trait of character. It marks the chastened spirit, the soul that has surrendered, the will that has been subdued, the heart that has learned to wait and sacrifice. This is one of the most valuable qualities of the highest Christian life.

Again it is translated "gentleness," the spirit of Christian refinement, free from harshness, rudeness, coarseness, unkindness, the spirit that is harmless as the dove and gentle as the soft breath of evening. This is always characteristic of the heart that is possessed by the heavenly Dove. It is also translated "humility," and there is no rarer or richer element in Christian loveliness than the lowly spirit, which has learned not so much to think less of itself as not to think at all of self; which takes its true place and never intrudes into another's; which never gets in the way of others, or asserts its self-importance, but leans, like John the beloved, on Jesus' breast, his face hidden on the Savior's bosom while the Master's alone is seen.

But the Syriac version has probably given us the most striking translation of this word. It is the word "sweetness." "Let your sweetness be known unto all men." It is that quality that probably blends all the qualities already named, and clothes us with the divine attractiveness that makes us a blessing to all we meet, a balm to the suffering, a rest to the weary, an inspiration to the depressed and a rebuke to the unkind. It is the quality which can "suffer long and be kind"; which can endure all with "great endurance and patience" (Colossians 1:11), and come through the flame without the smell of fire. We have seen it in some of His dear saints, and it was always manifest in Him. Let it be known unto all men. Do not hide it in your closet. Do not keep it for select occasions, but wear it as a beautiful garment. Shed it around you as a holy radiance. Take it into the bustling street until it breathes its fragrance on the agitated and excited ones around you. Carry it into the place where others wrong you or despise you, until it shall reprove them as your resentment never could. Show it to your enemies, and don't forget to show it to your friends. Pour it out in the home circle to husband, wife, child and friend, until all you meet shall feel as if a breath of summer and a gleam of sunshine had passed by. "Let your sweetness be known to all men."

Don't wait till people die to plant your flowers on their grave, but while they live shed the fragrance of love on their tired and tempted hearts. For all this the incentive and encouragement is given in the next brief sentence: "The Lord is near" (Philippians 4:5). Perhaps it means that the Lord is nearby watching you, testing you, ready to help and sustain you; and perhaps it means the Lord is coming soon, and all these trials will seem but little things in the light of that blessed hope and surpassing glory. "Let your sweetness therefore, be known to all men, for the Lord is at hand."

Peace

"And the peace of God, which transcends all understanding, will guard your hearts and your minds in Christ Jesus" (4:7). Peace is the most precious of all the gifts and graces of the Spirit; so precious indeed is peace that it was the one legacy left us by our departing Lord. "Peace I leave with you; my peace I give you. I do not give to you as the world gives. Do not let your hearts be troubled and do not be afraid" (John 14:27). Joy may be more exciting, but peace is more sustaining. Joy may be the wine of life, but peace is its refreshing water and its daily bread.

Let us look a little more closely at this precious gift.

1. It is God's peace.

It is the "peace of God." It is not peace with God, which comes to us with forgiveness and salvation, but is the very peace of God Himself—His own calm, restful heart possessing ours, and filling us with His divine stillness.

2. It transcends understanding.

It is a "peace of God, which transcends all understanding" (Philippians 4:7). There is no rational explanation of it. It does not come to us by reasoning things out, and seeing our way clear, but it is often most profound when all the circumstances of our life are perplexing and distressing. It contradicts all conditions and constantly proves its heavenly origin and its supernatural birth. It is indeed the peace of God, and as wonderful as was His own calm, tranquil spirit when standing on the threshold of the garden and the cross.

I remember a Christian woman, for a long time a member of my church, on whom there suddenly fell the greatest sorrow that can come to a loving heart. It was the death of her husband, the companion of half a century of happy wedded life. She was a quiet, practical woman, with no natural emotion or sentiment in her temperament. But she had received the Holy Spirit years before and, in a very calm, consistent way, had been living a very devoted life. Hastening to her home I expected to find her plunged in deep distress, but she met me at the door with radiant face and overflowing joy. "My dear pastor," she cried, "my family all think that I am wrong to feel as I do, for I cannot shed a tear, and my heart is so happy that I cannot understand it. God has filled me with such a peace as passes all understanding, and I really cannot help rejoicing and praising Him all the time. What shall I do?" Of course I told her to rejoice with all her heart, and thank God that she could rejoice in such an hour. It was indeed the peace that passed all understanding. There was no human cause for it. It was the deep artesian well flowing from the heart of God.

3. It saves us from care.

It is the peace that saves us from anxious care. Its watchword is "Do not be anxious about anything" (4:6). It simply crowds out all our corroding anxieties and fills us with such satisfaction that there is really nothing that we can fear. No, nothing. The command is unconditional and unlimited. "Do not be anxious about anything." Not even for your spiritual life. Not even for your friends. Not even for the answers to your prayers.

Not even for the highest and holiest things. Cast every burden on the Lord and trust everything with Him.

4. It leads to prayer.

It is a peace that leads to constant prayer and is sustained by a life of prayer. "But in everything, by prayer and petition, with thanksgiving, present your requests to God" (4:6). This does not mean that we are to be indifferent to the things that concern us or others, but that we are to be free from worry about them by handing them over to One who can attend to them better than we can, and who is already carrying the responsibility and the care. This is really the truest self-interest, to hand over our interest to a wisdom and a love superior to our own, and then we know that all must be well.

The word "supplication" is derived from a root that signifies "many ply." It refers to the minutiae of life and the innumerable details of life's cares and burdens, all of which we may bring, and bring again and again, to Him who cares for us, and then leave them at His feet and know that they are safe in His keeping.

5. It fills the heart with thankfulness.

It is a peace that fills the heart with constant thankfulness and the lips with praise. Our prayers are turned to praise, and as we thank Him for what we have, we have new cause for more thanksgiving. The surest way to receive answers to our prayers is to praise for what we have received, and then to praise for what we have not yet received. A life of peace leads to a life of praise, and a life of praise in turn leads to a life of peace. There are some natures that always see the dark side first. There are some that can see only the sunshine, the silver lining and the coming morning.

6. *It guards our heart.*

This peace is the guardian and the garrison of our heart. It keeps us, or, in the meaning of the Greek word, "garrisons" us, shutting out unhappy and unholy thoughts, and creating an atmosphere out of which only righteousness and blessing can spring.

7. *It keeps our heart and mind.*

It keeps our heart and mind—the heart first, and then the mind in consequence. It is not the mind first and then the heart, but it is heart foremost, that the sweetest Christian life always moves. Would you know the remedy for anxious, distracting and ill-regulated thoughts? It is a heart kept by the peace of God, and still as ocean's depths where the surging billows that toss the surface into angry foam never come. This is the very element and atmosphere where faith and love may dwell deep in the heart of God. This is "the peace of God, which transcends all understanding."

CHAPTER 7

Whatever Is Lovely

Finally, brothers, whatever is true, whatever is noble, whatever is right, whatever is pure, whatever is lovely, whatever is admirable—if anything is excellent or praiseworthy—think about such things. (Philippians 4:8)

This passage expresses the very point of the apostle's subject in this letter, and by one discriminating flash of light points out the difference between the essentials of holy character and the lighter touches of grace and loveliness which may be added to these.

Two classes of virtues are here specified, and each class is designated by a special word: "If anything is excellent" called fundamental and essential to holy character; "or praiseworthy," denotes those qualities, which, while not essential, are ornamental.

The first class includes three specifications, namely, "whatever is true, . . . whatever is right, whatever is pure." Without these there can be no morality and no religion. These are the cardinal virtues of life, the solid texture out of which the web is woven, the warp and woof on which the other qualities are embroidered as decorations and adornings.

The second class includes also three specifications. "Whatever is noble." This ought to be translated honorable, venerable, lofty, for it denotes not so much practical righteousness as rather the qualities that demand admiration and veneration. Next, "whatever is lovely," those qualities that are inherently beautiful and attractive, and make the possessor to be esteemed and beloved. The third specification is "whatever is admirable," or those things that constitute influence, reputation and public esteem and respect. These are objects of praise and are to be added to the others. The qualities of virtue are like the solid granite rock; the qualities of praise resemble the luxuriant forest, the verdant grass, the mossy banks, the blooming shrubs and flowers, the sparkling waterfalls that cover those substantial rocks and turn the desert into a garden of beauty and delight. Let us look at these two classes of moral qualities, but especially the second.

Moral Qualities

1. The essentials of character.

There are three essentials of character. The first is truth. Our religious character must be founded upon right principles, and having adopted them we must be true to them. Truth must be at once objective and subjective. We must have the truth, and we must be true to it. Sound doctrine must be held by a sound and sincere heart.

Next, "whatever is right," covers the whole range of our relationships to our fellowmen, our practical righteousness, our rightness of life in the family, in the social world, and in our business fellowships with others.

Finally, "whatever is pure," has reference to our own personal life. It describes a heart cleansed by the blood of Christ, filled with holy motives, thoughts and affections and leading to right relations toward all men and toward God. These are the essential qualities of the Christian life. Without them there can be no morality and no religion.

2. The graces of Christian character.

But next are the graces of Christian character, "the beauties of holiness" (Psalm 110:3, KJV), as the Old Testament expresses it. One may be a Christian without these, but not without those mentioned before. They are the refinements of holy character—the lesser touches by which perfection is attained. Even as the marble is polished by a thousand little touches. The difference between an ordinary copy and a work of genius lies in minute details which the coarse, uncultivated eye might never be able to detect.

Now, some of these graces are connected with the cardinal virtues already described. That is to say, there are people who may be said to be truthful, and who would not deliberately misrepresent, yet they will exaggerate, they will shade the truth by little touches and faint colorings which practically do misrepresent and mislead. Then, again, there are some who are, in the main, honest, just and righteous, and would not willfully or knowingly do another a wrong. Yet perhaps they are too careless or too keen, and by little touches of unrighteousness mar the testimony of their lives. Then there are others who are pure in their purpose and intent, but it may be in their dress, manners, deportment or conversation, compromise their influence enough to miss the full effectiveness of a holy life. Thus it becomes important to give heed to the message: "Do not allow what you consider good to be spoken of as evil" (Romans 14:16), and even in the things that are just and pure and true, to be careful to add the "things that are lovely" and "admirable."

Another Class of Qualities

But there is a distinct field, represented by another class of qualities altogether, which constitutes the graces and refinements of the holy life, and of which it is true "You should have practiced the latter without leaving the former undone" (Luke 11:42).

1. Dignity and Self-respect

Dignity and self-respect are the things that add to the weight of our character and influence and may be covered by the first phrase, "whatever is true," or rather, "venerable." The estimate which others place upon us will always be proportioned to our true estimate of ourselves. There is a great difference between conceit and self-respect. "Don't let anyone look down on you" (1 Timothy 4:12), is the dictate at once of true instinct and Holy Scripture. The Lord Jesus always bore Himself with true dignity, and allowed no person to be too familiar. Even the disciple that leaned upon His breast looked up to Him with sacred awe. We can be simple, unaffected and humble, and yet carry ourselves with the holy dignity of the sons and daughters of God. Paul was a fine example of true manliness. When unjustly imprisoned, he refused to sneak out and run away, but manfully answered, "They beat us publicly without a trial, even though we are Roman citizens, and threw us into prison. And now do they want to get rid of us quietly? No! Let them come themselves and escort us out" (Acts 16:37). The soul in which the Holy Spirit dwells will always carry itself with sacred loftiness, as well as sweet humility. This is the safeguard of woman, and the glory of man.

2. Necessary Modesty

Modesty is as necessary as dignity, and at once corrects it and adorns it. It does not lower our self-respect, but it simply veils us with the beautiful covering of self-unconsciousness. You may always know John, the beloved, by the fact that he never mentions himself, but speaks of the "disciple

whom Jesus loved" (John 13:23). When Moses'
face shone with the brightest glow, he did not
know that it shone at all. When beauty is conscious of itself it becomes disgusting. When talent
and genius begin to show off, then they sink be-
low contempt. When spiritual gifts and holy services are used to glorify the possessor or the
worker, then they become objects of derision and
lose their merit.

The seraphim not only covered their faces but
their feet with their wings, and tried to hide not
only their beauty but their work. God gives us the
sweetly chastened spirit that bows its head and
stands veiled with heavenly modesty.

3. *Personal Habits*

Personal habits have much to do with the loveliness of our character and our lives. While we do
not believe with that old lady that "cleanliness is
next to godliness," yet we certainly believe that
cleanliness stands near to godliness. While we do
not go so far as to denounce chewing, smoking
and snuffing as the basest of crimes, yet it is
enough to say that they are not among the things
that are lovely, venerable or of good report. And
there are a thousand other things which a sanctified soul will learn, by holy intuition and watch-
fulness, to lay aside as defects if not defilements.

4. *Refinement and Courtesy*

Good manners, refinement, and courtesy are
among the things that are lovely and attractive in

our Christian example. There is an affectation of refinement that is but the gloss and the counterfeit,
but the true follower of Jesus Christ will always be
gentle and gentlemanly, considerate of others and
careful to avoid offense, and will act toward all with
whom he comes in contact with that thoughtful
consideration and courteous politeness which speak
so strongly for Christ. After the greatest gentleman
in Europe, Lord Chesterfield, had spent a few days
with Archbishop Fénelon, who was as sweet as he
was saintly, he remarked, "If I had stayed much
longer I should have been charmed into accepting
his religion." "Be courteous" is one of the commands
of the Holy Spirit. The Christian lady and the
Christian gentleman will carry their good manners
into the kitchen and the factory, as well as into the
social circle; the wife will be as polite to her husband
and her cook as she is to the fashionable caller in the
afternoon. The parent will be as gentle and considerate in speaking to his child, as when called to receive some distinguished visitor, or in wearing some
courtly air on a great public occasion. Let us adorn
the little things and the commonplaces of life with
that "great . . . love," which "the Father has lavished
on us" (1 John 3:1), and which He would have us reflect.

5. *Propriety*

Propriety, good sense, and the instinct of knowing the fitness of things, and always acting with
good taste are among the most charming features
of a well-balanced character. It is what the apostle

calls, "the spirit . . . of a sound mind" (2 Timothy 1:7, KJV). The Lord Jesus was always on time and in order. We never find Him making a mistake or doing an unbecoming thing. And so of divine love it is said, "It is not rude, it is not self-seeking, it is not easily angered, it keeps no record of wrongs" (1 Corinthians 13:5). A very simple remark, if appropriate to the occasion, is more effective than the most eloquent speech which is out of place. The Holy Spirit will give the heavenly quality of doing the right thing at the right time and in the right manner.

6. *Fitting Speech*

A well-balanced character will display wise and fitting speech, a well-governed tongue and a discreet pen. Briefly, fitness in the use of words. This has much to do with the effectiveness of our lives and the attractiveness of our example. To be able to state in a few brief words the matter about which you wish to confer, to come quickly to the point and stop when you get there—what a rare gift! To be able to put on the first page of your letter the exact idea that you mean to express, and to get to the point of your subject before you exhaust the patience and interest of your correspondent, these are things that do not require so much education as consideration. The conversational bore not only wearies his listener, but must often weary the Lord Himself.

Such errors largely arise either from selfishness, self-consciousness or lack of consideration for others. These are little things, but they are the flies that spoil the ointment or the touches that polish the workmanship and glorify the grace of God. Reserve in conversation is just as necessary as frankness. "A fool gives full vent to his anger,/ but a wise man keeps himself under control" (Proverbs 29:11). There is a silence that is golden, and a quiet dignity that belongs to all spiritual force and that speaks for God in our very manner.

7. Cheerfulness of Disposition

Cheerfulness of disposition and manner have much to do with our influence and example. There are people who clasp your hand with a clammy touch that makes you think of a corpse. There are other touches that stir you, and looks that inspire you, and faces that lift you to heavenly things.

It is told of a Christian minister who was in deep depression, that while attending certain religious meetings in England he was attracted by the face of a lady who attended the services from day to day. Her calm and peaceful expression of countenance impressed him with a sense of the Lord's presence, and encouraged him to seek and obtain the baptism of the Holy Spirit and the same source of light and gladness which he saw reflected in her. Long afterwards he met her and told her how her silent look had been the benediction of his life. Our faces can speak for God; and, if the heart is illuminated within, we ought to show it in every feature, in every tone, in every gesture. Our whole expression and bearing should be such as to make men say of us, as they said of some of old, "Each one with the bearing of a prince" (Judges 8:18).

8. *Cordiality and Heartiness*

Cordiality and heartiness of spirit and manner are desirable. There are people that chill us and repel us, and there are others that draw us and encourage us. There is a stiffness that is sometimes born of diffidence, sometimes of selfishness, sometimes of natural coldness. But it can be overcome by a true spirit and by a watchful discipline.

Just as a graceful carriage can be acquired by thoughtful attention, and a careless, clumsy and clownish walk can grow upon one through carelessness and neglect, so we can accustom ourselves to such thoughtful and loving consideration of others as will transform our very manner, and make us, as the divine picture so beautifully characterizes it, "Be devoted to one another in brotherly love. Honor one another above yourselves" (Romans 12:10). "Finally, all of you, live in harmony with one another" (1 Peter 3:8). A very large part of our Christian life consists of our social and domestic relations and communication. It is in the little touches of love, kindness and mutual consideration that the spirit of Christ shines out most constantly; and the lack of it is often most painfully manifest.

9. *Sensitivity to Others*

Sensitiveness to the feelings of others is a beautiful quality often found wanting in good people. If they meet a poor consumptive, they will be very likely to tell him how dreadful he looks, throwing over him the shadow of the grave, until he feels as if he had been at his own funeral. If there is a sore place anywhere they are sure to step on it. If you have some peculiar and deep affliction, they are very likely to refer to it in some coarse and thoughtless manner, until you find relief in silent tears and hasten to shorten the painful interview.

True Christian sweetness adjusts itself to others. It rejoices with them that do rejoice, and weeps with them that weep. The law of love is its great impulse, and it is ever watching with kind consideration to avoid offenses on the one hand, and on the other to contribute to the happiness of all with whom we come in contact.

10. Tact

Tact is an indefinable quality, but we are very distinctly conscious of it when we see it, and we are often painfully sensible of its absence. Its possessor has a charmed life, and a golden secret that melts away difficulties, misunderstandings and angry countenances, as the gentle sunshine. A good-natured remark, a playful witticism, a happy change in the subject of conversation, a word that provokes a smile, how often these things have prevented the gravest misunderstandings and solved the hardest problems.

In dealing with souls it is essential to study our cases and adapt ourselves to conditions. "He who wins souls is wise" (Proverbs 11:30). A brusque address, an intrusive remark, an offensive question or a lot of tiresome talk, will do far more harm than good to the soul that you seek to benefit, and often retard for years the work of conviction that may have already begun. How delicately Christ dealt with the woman of Samaria, the publican of Jericho, and the dying thief upon the cross! If His Spirit dwells in us we shall have His wisdom and skill.

11. Others' Faults

In dealing with the faults of others there is room for the graces of Christian character. On the one hand there should be divine tenderness and gentleness. We are never fit to speak to others of their faults until our hearts are overflowing with love and free from resentment. Divine tact will always find some good thing to commend before we blame or criticize. On the other hand, there is a holy firmness and a righteous indignation which are just as becoming and necessary under certain circumstances, and which only the grace of the Holy Spirit can keep from becoming natural temper or unholy excess.

12. Loyalty to Truth

Loyalty to truth, to God, to the cause to which we are committed and to the friends that God has given us—these are qualities essential to the highest Christian character. They are rare, and their price is above rubies; they are the elements that

constitute heroism and lead to the noblest sacrifices and the brightest examples of human friendship or public patriotism.

13. *Self-sacrifice*

Self-sacrifice is among the things that are lofty,
and this alone can lift us to the noblest heights of
character and conduct. The mountaintops of sacred biography all reach their summits on some
Moriah height where something has been sacrificed for principle or for God: where Abraham
gave up his Isaac; or Mary poured out her costly
ointment; or David's heroes dashed through the
ranks of their foes, and gladly risked their lives to
bring back to their king their helmets filled with
the water of Bethlehem's well for which he
longed. This was the glory of the great apostle,
and the only way in which he could expect to earn
a prize. For preaching the gospel he tells us there
was no glory. That was simply duty. But for
preaching the gospel without charge there was a
chance of winning a crown, and this was the glory
of his life. God will give to every true life such opportunities for sacrifice and reward if we only desire to meet them. Thus alone can the jewels of
the eternal crown be won.

14. *Devoutness*

This is the spirit of prayer, communion, devo-
tion to God and seraphic love. It was the spirit of
John the Divine; of Fénelon, the medieval saint; of
Madame Guyon; the loving heart of Samuel

Rutherford; the holiness of Edward Payson; the spiritual zeal of Robert Murray McCheyne— all were lives that lived in the light of an open heaven and breathed the sweet fragrance of the land of Beulah. Devoutness is one of the things that are venerable, the things that are lovely, the things that are of good report which the humblest saint may emulate.

15. *Enthusiasm*

Enthusiasm is important. No soul can greatly influence others unless it is itself on fire. Personal magnetism is borne of intense feeling and profound interest in the object that we have chosen. It is a shining quality, and a resistless force in Christian character. It gives impulse to our work, and wings our thoughts and words with heavenly power.

16. *A Holy Ambition*

A holy ambition, a heavenly aspiration, a life of hope and lofty endeavor will lift us above earthly and common things and make our lives sublime. We are the children of eternity. We are the heirs of glory. We have in prospect a crown that does not fade away, and an existence transcendently grander than the highest possibilities of earthly hope. How noble, how glorious, how aspiring we should be! What a grandeur it should add to our thoughts, conceptions, imaginations, to our very faces and bearing, as we press on to the glorious prize with the Spirit of the Master reflected in our countenances, and the light of the opening heaven shining on our transfigured brow. So "May the favor of the Lord our God rest upon us" (Psalm 90:17), even "the splendor of his holiness" (96:9), with the dew of His youth.

So let us prove not only the things that are true and right and pure, but whatever things are honest, whatever things are lovely, whatever are admirable, let us think about these things. And let us put on not only the clean robes of holiness, but the wedding robes of beauty and glory for the Marriage of the Lamb.

CHAPTER 8

The Great Secret

For I have learned to be content whatever the circumstances. I know what it is to be in need, and I know what it is to have plenty. I have learned the secret of being content in any and every situation, whether well fed or hungry, whether living in plenty or in want. I can do everything through him who gives me strength. (Philippians 4:11–13)

There is a secret in everything. Back of the discoveries of genius, the inventions of art and the marvelous transformations of our modern commercial and industrial life, there is always hidden away in some gifted brain a mighty secret whose potential value may be estimated by millions and billions of dollars. The very process by which this sentence will be turned into type, by the simple touch on a keyboard, is one of the most marvelous secrets of modern machinery, the linotype. The wizard of electrical science, from his laboratory in New Jersey, is working out new secrets every year in the practical applications of the electric current. The patent office in Washington protects innumerable little secrets of inventions of all the processes of modern business and machinery.

In the higher realm of the spiritual world everything depends on knowing how to do it. Human morals have failed because they had not learned God's secret. The ancient philosophers had their outer and inner circles, their mysteries into which the few were initiated and their occult science and philosophy. But it was all a labyrinth of useless speculation, and had no power to lift humanity out of its helplessness and sinfulness. Only by divine revelation could the problem be solved and the mystery revealed.

The great apostle tells us that the secret has at last been made known. The Revised Version furnishes a striking and beautiful translation of the last part of our text. "I have learned the secret, . . . I can do all things through Christ who strengtheneth me" (4:12–13). It is not the first time that Paul speaks of this secret. In his Epistle to the Colossians, there is a striking passage in which he refers to the "mystery," literally the secret "that has been kept hidden for ages and generations, but is now disclosed to the saints. To them God has chosen to make known among the Gentiles the glorious riches of this mystery" (Colossians 1:26–27). And then he tells us what it is: "Christ in you, the hope of glory" (1:27).

This was the great trust committed to him to deliver to the world. It is an open secret, and yet it is only comprehended by those who enter into the "shelter of the Most High [and] rest in the shadow of the Almighty" (Psalms 91:1). It is to these that he whispers it in our beautiful text, as he tells them how, by a power beyond themselves, they can live out the beautiful ideal which he has been presenting to them in this exquisite epistle.

The Nature of the Secret

He does not leave us one moment in doubt about it. It is thus, "I can do everything through him who gives me strength" (Philippians 4:13). The literal translation of this verse adds much force to it. "I am strong for everything in *the endynamiting Christ*." The Greek root of this last phrase has acquired a peculiar significance. Dynamite denotes the most powerful of material forces. The apostle means that he has found a power outside of himself and beyond his own power, the infinite power of Christ, and that he has come into connection with this power in such a way that it has become available for his every need, and while in touch with it, he is strong for everything and for all things.

Let us carefully note that this power is all centered in a Person, namely, the living Christ. And it is only while one is in this Christ, abiding in Him, depending upon Him, drawing his life from Him, that he has the command of this all-sufficient strength. It is not merely through the Christ, but it is in the Christ; that is, in actual union with Him, that the strength comes. It is not that so much power is communicated to him to be at his own control and disposal as a dynamo or battery might be, but that the power remains in the person of Christ, and is shared by the believer only while he is in direct union and communion with the Lord Himself.

This, then, was Paul's mighty secret, that God had united him with the Lord Jesus as the living source of all possible blessing, strength and sufficiency, and that it was his privilege to draw from Him moment by moment the supply for all his needs, just as the human system derives life from the oxygen we breathe through the inhalation of air into our lungs.

The human mind has always been straining after some closer union with the divine powers, and ancient art is just an attempt to bring the gods down in the likeness of men through the sculpture, paintings and mythologies of ancient Greece. But all this was cold and unsatisfying, the outreaching of an arm too short to reach the heavenly help for which human hearts are fainting. Paul, however, had found the secret. Not a god in marble, in poetry or in the legendary stories of ancient mythology, but a God in human flesh, a God who had lived our life with all its trials and experiences, and who, now exalted to a spiritual and heavenly manhood, still comes to dwell in human hearts and relive His life in our actual experiences from day to day. It is not merely occasional help, but His constant life and presence. There is no part of our existence which He cannot touch.

There is no place in our varied experience where He cannot meet us. His humanity is as broad as ours, and His presence and touch as real and tender as in the old Galilean days. This is the secret of all-sufficiency—the friendship of Jesus, the indwelling life of Christ, our union heart to heart with One who, as no other friend could possibly do, lives out His very life in ours.

Beloved, have you learned this secret? To distrust yourself and fully trust Him? To cease from your own works and let Him work in you to will and to do of His good pleasure?

The Application of this Secret

1. It is universal.

It applies to all things. It is a universal secret, and covers the whole range of our life and need. It extends to our spirit, our soul and our body, to our temporal as well as to our religious interest, to our families and friends as well as to ourselves, to our business, our circumstances, our health, our life, our death, our whole eternity. It is a universal secret.

2. It is particular.

It applies to everything, as well as to all things. It is particular, as well as general. It must be applied moment by moment to all the details of life. It is not something to think about in church, at communion seasons, on birthdays and anniversaries, at morning and evening prayer and on the great occasions of trial and need. But it is something that comes afresh with every breath, and that in order to be effectual must be constantly employed and applied in every separate link in the whole chain of human life, 60 seconds in the minute, and 24 hours in the day. This is where we often fail. We try to live wholesale lives. God's method is moment by moment, breath by breath, line upon line, here a little and there a little. We find, alas, too often that the chain is no stronger than its weakest link, and that the stitches we have dropped, the links we have lost, have destroyed the effectiveness of life as a whole.

3. It is self-contained.

It is a self-contained secret. There is a fine expression in the original translation of the word rendered "content" in our Revised Version. It is not exactly content, but rather self-sufficient or self-contained. "I have learned in all circumstances to be sufficient in myself." The idea is for the Christian to be independent of circumstances, and to have a source of satisfaction and comfort in his own soul that lifts him above the things outside of him. "My mind to me a kingdom is," is the human way of expressing independence of character and sufficiency of source. Much higher is the inspired statement of the greater truth, "The kingdom of God is within you" (Luke 17:21), and "The kingdom of God is not a matter of eating and drinking, but of righteousness, peace and joy in the Holy Spirit" (Romans 14:17).

One of our wisest Christian workers, recently addressing a party of missionary candidates, advised them not to go to the foreign field unless they had sufficient spiritual resources to make them happy within their own hearts even in loneliness and isolation. If you are going to be fretting in six months on account of homesickness or lonesomeness don't go to China. But if you have a Christ and a joy that make you happy in the loneliest place, quite independently of the things around you, then you can be happy anywhere and at leisure from your own cares to work effectively for God.

Now this was what Paul meant when he talked about being self-sufficient in every condition. He had within himself a kingdom of peace and joy that mere outward things could not disturb.

This expression was a technical term with the ancient Stoics. They were fond of talking about their independence of circumstances and things. Their philosophy taught them to despise circumstances and material gratifications, and they were able to maintain the form of outward stoicism, even as the Indian could stand at the stake with countenance unblanched amid all the terrors of a violent death. But this was only apparent. The heart was clinging to a shadow and really holding on to itself. The apostle meant something different from this; not merely the resolution of a firm, determined will, but the restful satisfaction of a heart filled with the peace and joy of the Lord, and finding its heaven within. This Christ can give, and in His perfect peace the heart can sing:

Everything in Jesus,
And Jesus everything.

4. *It is sufficient.*

This secret is sufficient for the severest trials and the deepest depression. "I know what it is to be in need" (Philippians 4:12), he exclaims, "I have learned how to be hungry. I know how to suffer need." All this he had proved by the severest experiences through which a human life has ever passed. There was no sort of trial that he had not proved, and yet his secret had stood the test. Look at him on the tossing deck of the vessel in the Mediterranean, the only bright and fearless spirit in all that company. Look at him chained to the soldier in the Roman barracks, rejoicing that he is permitted to bear testimony for Christ to the rude men around him. Listen to him as he bids farewell to his weeping friends at Ephesus, expressing the one ambition to finish his course with joy. Sometimes we see his spirit sinking just enough to put him in touch with his suffering brethren and have them know that he understands their trials and afflictions. The only time his spirit seems to break is when he is thinking of others and suffering for their sakes. For himself his spirit is always victorious, and he did indeed finish his course with joy, and prove to the end that Christ was all-sufficient for the most tried and suffering life.

How often people succeed under favorable circumstances and break down when trial comes. Tropical plants cannot stand the breath of frost.

God has to expose every life to the fire, and only that which stands the fire of trial can have a part in the final reward.

5. *It is equal to the test.*

His secret was equal to the severer test of prosperity. More difficult to stand even than trial, is happiness and success. Many a soul that has stood with fortitude amid the storms of adversity has sunk into soft and languid weakness under the enervating of prosperity and the world's approval. The wealth for which you longed has come, but the liberal heart has gone. The opportunities for usefulness for which you craved have been bestowed upon you, but the unselfish and obedient spirit which would have once improved them has disappeared. The holy courage that stood for God when others quailed, cannot now afford to sacrifice the good opinion of a world whose smile has proven too sweet for your once high purpose and principle. The world has become so necessary for your happiness that you cannot sacrifice it, and the work that once was strong in God in the day of small things is now, alas, like Laodicea, "rich; [having] acquired wealth and [not needing] a thing" (Revelation 3:17). But alas, the Master is standing at the door and saying, "You do not realize that you are wretched, pitiful, poor, blind and naked" (3:17).

This is not necessary. The grace of Christ is able to sustain the heart in the highest as well as the lowest place, to fill you with humble thankfulness for the prosperity that is but a trust for God, and to make you a faithful steward of the means and resources which He has bestowed upon you only that you might use them for Him. And so there are gifts without pride, of spiritual blessings that have not separated us from the Giver, of five talents that have been multiplied into ten, and of trusts so used for God that they have been increased a hundredfold.

You will notice in this classification the great variety of extremes covered by this experience. It is a secret that is equally applicable to the most opposite conditions of life.

The Brooklyn Bridge, it is said, contracts and expands with winter cold and summer heat nearly two feet in its entire length. But the great iron strands are adjusted so as to slip past each other on the mighty towers and allow for these extremes. More perfect is God's adjustment for the vicissitudes of His people. There is an inward life that is unmoved alike by heat and cold, a fixed and steadfast principle that presses on through the darkness and the light, through Him who is its source, "the same yesterday and today and forever" (Hebrews 13:8).

The Learning of this Secret

Three times the apostle refers to his spiritual education. First he says, "I have learned" (Philippians 4:11). Then he adds later, "I know" (4:12). And finally he tells us, "I am instructed" (4:12, KJV). This last expression is translated in the new version, "I have learned the secret"; and in one of the best versions it is, "I have been initiated."

There are really two stages in learning this great secret. The first is the acquiring of the principle. The second is the practice of its application, until we become perfectly familiar with its use and thoroughly proficient in its application.

To take a familiar illustration: in the art of phonography the principle is soon acquired. In a few days you can learn the characters and the general principles. But it takes months and sometimes years of patient application to be able to use them quickly and efficiently. And so we can soon comprehend the great principle of the spiritual life, the indwelling Christ and the Holy Spirit. We can very soon, if our hearts are true and sincere, begin the deeper life and receive the Holy Spirit.

But it is a very different thing to take this deep secret and apply it moment by moment to all the details of holy living. It is here that we constantly fail. At some consecration meeting, at some sacred altar, you gave yourself to Christ and received Him as your life and strength. But that was but the start. It is the abiding that tells. It is walking with Him step by step that makes Him real and proves His all-sufficiency. Alas, many of us are satisfied with a mere smattering of the holy art of walking with God. What we need is what an old writer calls "The practice of the presence of God"—the constant, patient, ceaseless dependence upon Him for everything; the applying of our secret to every test that comes in life, to every moment of every day until we can say with the great apostle, "I have been initiated, I have been instructed, I can do all things through him who gives me strength."

Beloved, shall we take this mighty secret, and go out to live it step by step and day by day, until we have walked through "the length and breadth of the land" (Genesis 13:17); and until, in the all things and the everything, the always and the everywhere, we shall have proved "what God's will is—his good, pleasing and perfect will" (Romans 12:2).

CHAPTER 9

The Boundless Sufficiency

And my God will meet all your needs according to his glorious riches in Christ Jesus. (Philippians 4:19)

There are some souls that always seem to be kept on scant measure. Their spiritual garments are threadbare, their faces pinched and their whole bearing is that of people who are poverty stricken and kept on short allowance. They are always "hard up," and on "the ragged edge" of want and bankruptcy. To use the vivid figure of Job they come through by "the skin of [their] teeth" (Job 19:20). Or as Paul expresses it in a stronger figure, they are "saved . . . as by fire" (1 Corinthians 3:15, KJV). They are represented in Bunyan's glorious dream, not by sturdy Christian, buoyant Hopeful, and heroic Faithful, but by poor old Ready to Halt, with his crutches, Mr. Much Afraid, with his downcast look, and Miss Despondency, with her long and miserable face.

They sing sometimes, but it is generally this:

Tis a point I long to know,
  Oft it causes anxious thought,
Do I love the Lord or no,
  Am I His or am I not?

And when they go to the prayer meeting their usual cry is, "Pray for me." They are always begging, always hungry, always waiting for somebody to help them, and seldom looking for a chance to help. Like Pharaoh's lean cows, they eat everything in sight, but still they are always half starved.

Loved? Yes, they are loved and cared for by the dear Lord, loved as the crippled child, as the invalid member of the family. Saved? Yes, they are saved through the exceeding grace of Jesus Christ, "He is able to deal gently with those who are ignorant and are going astray" (Hebrews 5:2). But they never can be samples of the King's household, representatives of His grace or attractions to draw men to His fold. They are poor, half-starved sheep that cast reflection on the goodness and the care of the Shepherd, and not happy, well-fed lambs that "lie down in green pastures" (Psalm 23:2) for very satiety, and make others feel like saying, "The LORD is my shepherd, I shall not be in want" (23:1). On the contrary many who look at them will say, "If that is Christianity, save me from it."

In contrast with such as these, there is another type of Christian character that we might call the "life more abundant." It is a life which overflows in thankful joy and unselfish blessing to others. Its faith is full assurance. Its love "always protects, always trusts, always hopes, always perseveres" (1 Corinthians 13:7), and "never fails" (13:8). Its patience has "longsuffering with joyfulness" (Colossians 1:11, KJV). Its peace "transcends all understanding" (Philippians 4:7). Its joy is "an inexpressible and glorious joy" (1 Peter 1:8). Its service is so free and glad that duty is delight and work a luxury of love. Its giving is not only cheerful but "hilarious." Its sacrifice is so willing that even pain is joy, if borne for others and for God. It has enough and to spare, and its love and joy find their outlet in giving the overflow to others and finding that "it is more blessed to give than to receive" (Acts 20:35).

In a word it has got out into the infinite as well as the eternal, and sails on the shoreless and fathomless sea of God and His infinite grace.

What a difference! It is the difference between the barren desert and the luxuriant oasis with waving palms and glorious verdure. It is the difference between the gaunt and hungry flock and the herds that lie down in green pastures and beside the still waters. It is the difference between the poor burdened horse that is trying to drag you up the hill, and the flying locomotive that carries you without an effort. It is the difference between the old pump by the roadside, out of which you could force a few pailfuls of water after you had poured one in, and the deep artesian well that pours its gushing torrent forth in floods. It is the difference between the viewless plain and the mountain landscape looking far out to the regions beyond and the "land of far distance." It is the difference between the shallow stream, where your boat every moment touches sand or strikes some hidden rock, and the deep unfathomable sea, where your keel never strikes bottom and you ride in safety amid the ocean's wildest swells.

Oh, the difference of these two lives.

> Once 'twas painful trying,
>   Now 'tis perfect trust;
> Once a half salvation,
>   Now the uttermost.
> Once I hoped in Jesus,
>   Now I know He's mine;
> Once my lamps were dying,
>   Now they brightly shine.

Let us look at Paul's testimony of this overflowing life.

In His Own Experience, It Was His Life

"I have received full payment," he cries, "I am amply supplied" (Philippians 4:18). Was there ever such a paradox?

A prisoner chained between two soldiers in a cheerless Roman barracks! A man who says, "I have suffered the loss of all things!" A hated, persecuted outcast, even now awaiting a trial in which his very life hung by a thread on the capricious will of the Roman tyrant! A man who bore in his body the scars of beatings, scourgings, shipwrecks and privations of every kind, and who, only a few days before, had received some scanty offering of clothing, food and perhaps a little money from his congregation in Philippi. It is this man who cries, "I have received full payment and even more" (4:18).

Was it a dream of a diseased imagination? Or was it true in some higher sense than the world could understand?

Yes, he had a life whose sources were not in circumstances or things. And that life was full and satisfying. He had a salvation proportioned to the depth of his sin and need and he could say of it, "The grace of our Lord was poured out on me abundantly, along with the faith and love that are in Christ Jesus" (1 Timothy 1:14). He had a hope of which he could boast, "For I am convinced that neither death nor life, neither angels nor demons, neither the present nor the future, nor any powers, neither height nor depth, nor anything else in all creation, will be able to separate us from the love of God that is in Christ Jesus our Lord" (Romans 8:35-39). He had a love that could say, "So I will very gladly spend for you everything I have and expend myself as well. If I love you more, will you love me less?" (2 Corinthians 12:15). He had a victory of which he could boast, "No, in all these things we are more than conquerors through him who loved us" (Romans 8:37). His sacrifices were so gladly made that he could say, "But even if I am being poured out like a drink offering on the sacrifice and service coming from your faith, I am glad and rejoice with all of you" (Philippians 2:17). His sufferings so little disturbed him that he could say, "I only know that in every city the Holy Spirit warns me that prison and hardships are facing me. However, I consider my life worth nothing to me, if only I may finish the race and complete the task the Lord Jesus has given me— the task of testifying to the gospel of God's grace" (Acts 20:23–24).

There was not one small thing about him. His whole character was built on the most colossal mold. He was a great, magnanimous soul, with a spiritual life as large as the heart of God. He could say to the Corinthians, "We are not withholding our affection from you, . . . open wide your hearts also" (2 Corinthians 6:12–13). Into this little, sorrow-beaten frame God compressed the grandest character that ever followed Jesus, and standing on the battlements of his sublime exaltation he tells us we may have all he had, and cries, "My God will meet all your needs according to his glorious riches in Christ Jesus" (Philippians 4:19).

For Others

Paul's life was an overflow life, and that always means a life that reaches out to bless others. It has enough and to spare for a suffering world and "grows rich in giving." Paul lived in the hearts of others. "I long to see you" (Romans 1:11), he wrote in anticipation of his visit to Rome. Not that he might see the splendid capital of the Caesars, nor even that he might enjoy the fellowship of his cherished friends, but "that I may impart to you some spiritual gift" (1:11). "We loved you so much," he writes to the Thessalonians, "that we were delighted to share with you not only the gospel of God but our lives as well" (1 Thessalonians 2:8).

The sufferings of the children of God were his. "Who is led into sin" (2 Corinthians 11:29), he writes to the Corinthians, "and I do not inwardly burn" (11:29)? His prayers are all for others. Rarely do we find him asking anything for himself. His life was all given away in ministry for others. And it was Christ he ministered. He had a Christ he could give away and yet retain. He was so filled with the Spirit of the Master that he could just pour out His life into every empty and open heart.

How blessed to find, how blessed to live such lives. How delightful it is to come in contact with hearts that are not preoccupied with their own needs, but are at leisure to lift the burdens of other hearts and help men to touch His garment.

Beloved, have you this glorious fullness? Have you gotten beyond your own self-consciousness, your own prayers, your own little circle of friends and family ties, until your heart is in touch with the Savior's and the world's? This is the crowning glory of the sweetest Christian life.

A heart at leisure from itself
To soothe and sympathize.

The Source of this Superabundant Life

It all came from the revelation and conception he had of God. He was but drinking at a higher fountain, and pouring out the fullness he received. He had found a heavenly spring, and he was but leading others to the same fountain.

The scantiness or the fullness of your life all depends upon how large a God you have! The God of most Christians is not much larger than the dumb idol of wood or stone the heathen worships and then takes down from its pedestal and scolds if it does not answer his prayers or meet his expectations. The God of Paul was a very glorious and mighty Being, and it was the greatness of his God that gave greatness to his character and life. He was but a vessel to receive and reflect the glory of God.

"The people that do know their God shall be strong and do exploits" (Daniel 11:32, KJV). The souls that have learned to clothe themselves with His Almightiness are the people of enlarged vision and victorious faith. Human heroes are honored for what they have become or achieved. God's heroes are honored for the measure in which they have dropped out of sight and simply magnified Him. It is not Elijah but Elijah's God that we remember. It is not Paul, but Paul's Christ that we want.

What then does Paul mean when he says, "My God"?

1. The God of Nature

He means the God of nature. The God who shall fully supply all our need is the God who made the heavens and earth and upholds the whole system of the universe by the hand that once hung from the nails of Calvary. Look at the glory of the heavens and the elements of nature. Multiply every star you see in yonder heavens by 100 and you have not begun to count the worlds of space, but He made them all. They are poised by His power and moved by His omnipotence. In perfect order and awful might they sweep along their orbits through immensity. Yonder in the cluster of the Pleiades that little star is 12,000 times the size of our sun. And there are millions of such suns all along the heavenly fields, each surrounded by systems and satellites. Cannot He who holds them in His hand supply all your need?

2. The God of the Old Testament

He is the God of the Old Testament. He is the El Shaddai of Abraham, the great I AM of Moses, the Captain of Joshua's vision, the Jehovah God of Elijah's miracles, the mighty Providence of Esther and Nehemiah, the God who divided the sea, marched through the wilderness, shattered the walls of Jericho, halted the sun at Joshua's command, raised the dead at Elijah's word, stilled the lions for Daniel's protection, walked through the fire with the Hebrew children and proved equal to all His people's needs through 4,000 years of Old Testament history—history of patriarchs, prophets and saints. Is not the God of Abraham, of Esther, of Daniel, of Elijah, able to supply all your need?

3. The Father of Jesus Christ

He is the God and Father of our Lord and Savior Jesus Christ. The life of Jesus is just the expression of His power and love. He stood among men healing the sick, pardoning sinners, comforting the sad—doing it all in the Father's name and by His authority and will. "My Father is always at his work to this very day, and I, too, am working" (John 5:17), was His constant testimony. "My miracles of power, My words of grace, are just My Father's will, My Father's love." The God who so loved the world as to give His one and only Son (3:16), this is the God who "will meet all your needs according to his glorious riches in Christ Jesus" (Philippians 4:19).

4. The God of the Risen Christ

He is the God of the risen Christ. He is the God for whom even death has no barrier that can hinder His purpose or defy His will. He who burst asunder the bars of the grave, and without an effort passed through that sealed stone and met His sorrowing disciples with the glad "All Hail" of the first Easter morning, He it is who will supply all our need according to "his incomparably great power . . . which he exerted in Christ when he raised him from the dead" (Ephesians 1:19–20).

5. The God of the Ascension

He is the God of the ascension. Not only did He raise Him from the dead, but He "seated him at his right hand in the heavenly realms, far above all rule and authority, power and dominion, and every title that can be given, . . . and appointed him to be head over everything for the church"

(1:20–22). He is enthroned above all other power. He controls every force in the universe. And He is yours. Can He not supply your need?

6. *The Great Intercessor*

He is the great Intercessor. He is in heaven as our Advocate, Representative and Friend. His one business is to hear our petitions, present them to His Father, and send us the answers. We have a right to His constant intervention and efficient aid. With such a Friend what can we ever need, how can we ever fail?

7. *The God of Heaven*

He is the God of heaven. What do we know of heaven? How much does that expression mean to us, "his glorious riches" (Philippians 4:19)? Something we may gather from the inspired descriptions of that City that has no need of the sun, whose walls are jewels and its streets are shining gold—that glorious New Jerusalem, whose countless streets shall stretch for 1,500 miles north and south and east and west, and then as high up in mid-heaven, for the length, the breadth and the height of it are equal. And surely He who can build that Golden City is rich enough to supply all your need. Sometimes as the gates have parted to let some loved one in we have caught a glimpse of its surpassing glories; and we have felt, oh, if He has all this for us by and by can He not supply all our present needs, and anticipate a little our coming heritage of glory? O beloved, how ashamed we shall be some day that we did not better understand our heavenly calling and walk more truly "with the bearing of a prince" (Judges 8:18).

Yes, this is some feeble measure of "his glorious riches" (Philippians 4:19), and it is according to this that He will supply all our need. Let us trust Him. And let us clothe ourselves with His all-sufficiency and rise to the grandeur of His glorious fullness.

Finally, how shall all this be ours?

First, we must learn to say *my* God.

And secondly, we must learn to understand that "our every need" is just the vessel He is ever sending to hold His fullness. Let us pass down the little buckets of need on the endless chain of faith and prayer, and they will come up brimming with His overflowing fullness, each one saying as it flows: "My God will meet all your needs according to his glorious riches in Christ Jesus" (4:19).